SAPLINGS
AND
ROOTS

(TWO FACETS OF HINDUISM)

by
D. R. Sharma
LITTLE INDIA FOUNDATION, CHICAGO

COSMOS PUBLISHING

Published by :
Cosmos Publishing
P. O. Box 2913
Cedar Park
Texas 78630

© D. R. Sharma

ISBN 0-9663404-2-6

Library of Congress
Catalog Number 99-072270

October 1999

Printed by :
Anant V. Joshi
Sahitya Mudranalay
1263, Sadashiv Peth
Pune 411 030.
(INDIA)

To all noble souls who have contributed towards

enhancing the sense, dignity and pride in our heritage

And

To the coming generations of Hindus

in the West who have to carry it forward.

For my interest in Vedanta I owe a great deal to the river Ganges and to my father. He started me on Bhagavad Gita and Upanishads (two thirds of *prasthāntrayi*) as soon as I was able to read and write. My native village is on the riverbank and *sanyāsis* passed through constantly spending a few days there in the course of their wanderings. Traditionally, a *sanyāsi* would stop his wandering during the rainy season and stay in one place. The village must have some special charm since every year a *sanyāsi* would spend the season (*chāturmāsa*) in a hut on the riverbank. In the evenings my father went to see those holy men dragging me along, I had no choice. The discussions would go on for hours, at least it seemed to me so. I understood precious little, if anything, of the discussions or the scriptures. Yet I must have picked up quite a bit subconsciously. But for that start I would not be writing this book.

Much later in life I was fortunate enough to meet another *sanyāsi* and develop a relationship close to friendship. Many of the ideas expressed in this book crystallized during informal discussions with late Swami Tilak over a period of several years.

Finally, the publication of this book would not have been possible without the untiring efforts of Dr. Jayant Mandlik and encouraging support from other members of the Little India Foundation.

FOREWORD

The cultural heritage is a gift - the very first one that God chose to bestow upon us. To lose it knowingly or unknowingly is to ignore His wish. In a rapidly changing world, where opportunities take people far from their lands of origin, the task of maintaining one's cultural identity has become much harder. This is the problem facing Hindus immigrating to the West. The pace of immigration started accelerating decades ago and it was obvious that the Hindu Community in general had to devise some means to maintain continuity through future generations and preserve its heritage without isolating itself from the society in which it lived. It was with this in mind that we formed the Little India Foundation - a nonprofit organization in Chicago area in the seventies to teach Hindu children the basic values of their religion and culture. There were no temples and professional priests at that time, so the Foundation also catered to the needs of the community by providing competent individuals to perform various rites. Regular meetings with children of different age groups were held, not as classes but as informal discussion groups. Most of the children at that time had spent their early years in India, so they had some idea about what we were talking about. But even then, they had acquired the attitude of not accepting anything unquestioningly. It became apparent that the basics of Hinduism had to be taught to them in conformity with the modern world in which they lived and the need for a book like the present one was perceived even then.

Today the community has grown much larger and many of the children, including those in colleges, have been born and brought up here. Meanwhile there are parents who themselves do not have a clear concept of the basics of Hinduism and, therefore, can not teach their children. With the growth of the community, temples have been built and various organizations have started classes for children. But one pressing need is to provide to the children a rational basis for things that we want them to believe in. And this can be done, since the basic tenets of Hinduism transcend space and time and it has an inherent ability to adapt itself to new circumstances.

The present book illustrates that and offers parents as well as grown up children an opportunity to see the religion as a part of life well beyond what it may appear on the surface. It will also serve as an excellent textbook for courses on Hinduism or on comparative religions. This is the first of a series of books and the Foundation is striving to bring valuable information to the community through books, newsletter, and the Internet.

S.C. Soni, MD
Joliet, Illinois
President
Little India Foundation
Chicago.
‹scsoni@webtv.net›

June 9, 1999

PREFACE

Over twenty years ago we had started Little India Foundation for children of first generation Hindu immigrants with the intention of making them aware and proud of their religion and culture. It soon became apparent that the children growing up in this environment were not willing to accept some of our beliefs just on faith. While they are very young they may obey the parents and do whatever they are asked to, but as they grow older they do not want to do things just because they are told to; they need to be convinced that those are the right things to do. They do not want to believe in things that they can not rationalize to themselves. In schools and among friends they realize that they are different and shy away from saying or doing something that might provoke alienation. At home they may begin to have doubts regarding some aspects of the religion and culture that parents try to tell them. This problem is compounded by the fact that many parents do not themselves have a clear concept of the basics, or are unable to explain to their children in a rational way. There are supernatural aspects in all religions. Hinduism being so rich and diverse in philosophy as well as practice, superhuman phenomena are in abundance. This makes the children more susceptible to doubts and they begin to question the reality of the things that they are asked to learn. Given this situation and the fact that the fate of the religion in the new country of adoption depends on future generations, it is critical to explain to the children the basics of Hinduism at their level. Parents and the community have to realize that it is their responsibility to inculcate into the children the required knowledge, and through that a sense of pride in their heritage. The need for written material to help parents and also young inquisitive minds in this regard became clear even at that time.

In the past few years there have been efforts to teach children the basic values through formal classes and special programs. Some international organizations have made children's schools a part of their program. Individual communities have also started Sunday schools for this purpose. These efforts are laudable but we have to realize that the main responsibility still remains with the parents. A class once or even a few times a week is not going to do much good if the parents do not get involved in the process on a day to day basis. And for this to be effective the parents themselves must have a good knowledge of the basics of Hinduism. At first it is the ritualistic aspect that the child is exposed to and it is through the visual perception that he learns about the religion. At this stage it is important that the rituals are explained to the child as being symbolic representations of one's feelings towards God and not just mechanical gestures. It is in the formative years that the interest in and inquisitiveness towards the religion can be inculcated. As the young ones grow, the philosophical aspect can be taught to them gradually at their own level. When they reach an age at which they can read and understand things by themselves, all they need is occasional guidance. The philosophical aspect of Hinduism ranges from very simple to highly complex and abstract notions. Once the young mind grasps the basics, it can continue delving deep into the philosophy at its own pace.

This book addresses primarily the needs of Hindu parents and young adults living outside India but it can equally well serve the needs of anyone desirous of learning the basic facts underlying the philosophy and practice of Hinduism. For those willing to delve deeper into the subject, there are enough pointers to lead them on. An attempt has been made to present a complete picture covering both ritualistic and philosophical aspects, emphasizing the fact that for the most part the two are convergent. A common misconception about Hinduism, especially in the West, is that it is polytheistic and a religion of idol worshipers. But behind the apparent multiplicity of gods there has been a common thread of monism embedded in the religion all through its history. Behind every deity there is the backdrop of one omnipotent, omnipresent, omniscient God without form, without attributes. The deity is only a symbolic representation of some aspect of that One which the devotee chooses to worship. It is the same thing with idols. We do not worship the idol, we worship the deity (and through him some particular aspect of God) that it represents. No one in his right mind will ever think that gods are made of stone or whatever material the image is made of. The image is not god any more than a flower painted on canvass is fabric. Just as the photograph of a person helps one conjure his personality, the image helps to think of and concentrate on God; it is simply an aid. Every thought is associated with some image; this association is inherent to human nature. If we get to the roots, Hinduism has the most abstract concept of God — He is not a person one can approach and fall on His feet; God is a state of existence. If a man can continually improve himself and attain perfection, he has reached that exalted state and become one with God — he has attained nirvana.

In certain respects Hinduism is unique — very different from other major religions of the world. It was not started by a particular person but grew out of collective spiritual experiences of a large number of sages over several centuries. In Hinduism God has no form and no attributes, so He can be worshipped in any form we choose — man, woman, child — whatever. One has freedom to choose one's own personal god realizing that the personal god is only a partial representation of the one God. Hinduism has no commandments, no dogmas. Any do's and dont's that appeared later, were concocted by vested interests to perpetuate their hold over the masses. It is the only religion that puts man on par with God, regarding the soul as an infinitesimal part of the super-soul that is God. No other religion has given man so much freedom as to call himself God *(Aham Brahmāsmi)*. With freedom comes also the responsibility and in spite of all the problems besetting Hinduism, Hindus have behaved responsibly throughout history. It is the only religion that does not believe in proselytizing and conversion. There are any number of reasons for us to feel proud of our religion and culture. If we can get this idea across to our future generations, Hinduism will not only survive, it will thrive.

November 10, 1998   **D. R. Sharma**

Cedar Park, Texas

CONTENTS

Appendix A   : Gems from Religious Books

Appendix B   : Catering to the Intellect
                             Narrative and Philosophy

List of Illustrations :
(1) Om   (2) Swastika.
(3) Ten directions (4) Brahmā
(5) Vishnu   (6) Shiva
(7) Natarāj   (8) Saraswati
(9) Laxmi   (10) Pārvati
(11) Ganesha   (12) Rāma
(13) Krishna   (14) Durgā
(15) Kāli

PART ONE

PART ONE

CHAPTER ONE

WORSHIP — WHAT, WHY AND HOW

There is one fundamental concept common to every religion on earth — God created the universe. The differences arise when we consider who created religion. In spite of the differences, however, it is safe to say that man created religion. Man was not bestowed with religion, it came as an inherent need of the human race as it developed. God also created one earth, man subsequently divided it into parts — a process that seemingly has no end. A child is not born with a religion, he is born into a religion. Isolated from the parents he has no religion, no identity. The desire for progeny arises from an instinctive urge on the part of the parents for perpetuating their lineage that includes the religion and culture. The future of any society and its religion depends on how well subsequent generations are connected to the past and that, in turn, depends on how effective the parents and the society are in imparting their values and beliefs to the children. It is not an easy task and becomes more difficult when the parents get uprooted and have to bring up their children in entirely different social surroundings. This is the task that the Hindus immigrating to the West are faced with.

Hindu children growing up in communities outside India might have asked themselves over and over again what is this worship ritual that the parents make them sit through or what is worship. Some might follow the parents without questioning, others might have rebelled. As these children grow up in an environment where peer pressure works against the family influence, it is essential that we explain to them the rationale behind the rituals taking them beyond the mechanical aspect. Only then they can understand and feel proud of their heritage. The fate of Hinduism abroad lies in their hands. We need to explain to them the actions and their significance at their level.

The word worship means a reverent love and respect for someone or something. It is natural for human beings to have someone to look up to with love and respect. We find this all around us — in families, communities, countries and so on. At the very beginning man looked around and saw the sun, the moon, and the stars. He saw the precision with which day and night come, the seasons alternate. He saw the beauty of nature — how a tiny seed turns into a huge tree, the flowers bloom, the fruit ripens and finally produces the tiny seeds again. He also observed the forces of nature — the fire, the wind, the water, and their awesome power. Then he asked himself — who created all this, and not coming up with a direct answer concluded that there must be a hidden power behind the creation. Man could not see this Super Being but He was there all around him. He called this power God and looked up to Him as the ultimate object of reverence. With time different societies and cultures developed in the world and formed slightly different ideas about the specific nature of God and the creation of the world but the original concept remained as the universal background. Some cultures viewed different aspects of God reflected in nature in the form of visible objects like the sun, the fire, the wind, the water and saw in these elements God-like qualities; they began to revere these as gods. In course of time different philosophies and religions developed based on the way people perceived God in relation to man and adopted different ways of dealing with this new aspect of their lives. In some the reverence for God arose from an inner urge to understand the mysteries of the universe created by Him as well as of the Self that was an integral part of it. In others it grew out of a sense of fear that results from an awareness of one's own faults and shortcomings and from the realization that if God could create, He also had the capacity to destroy. This led to the concept of sinner and saviour in the relationship of man with God. Thus man looked up to God as the highest authority calling Him Lord and started paying homage to Him. This act was called worship.

The next question that may come to mind is why worship. The motivation for worship is different for different people. But one common element is faith; the person must have faith based on inner conviction. The ultimate objective of worship in any religion is to become a better person. Worship is like a staircase, it helps you to elevate yourself one step at a time. However, many people worship with the hope of material gains, be it wealth, health or progeny. There is nothing wrong in doing so as long as it is done with sincere devotion. Even if a person starts this way and keeps going, ultimately the desire for the material benefits falls by the wayside and he keeps moving up. The reason for worship depends also on the individual's attitude towards life and the stage of life he is at; he may worship with no motives at all. For most people, though, the motivation is to make their lives better. Everyone worshiping God is desirous of something. Wise men who have had spiritual awakening worship God and meditate on Him to realize His true nature; for them this is an inherent need for self-fulfillment. The seeker of knowledge wants to get to the ultimate truth for which his soul yearns and he comes to God in the search of that truth. The seeker of enjoyments comes to God after realizing the futility of seeking material pleasures and disillusioned by their transient nature. Lastly, those who are in distress and have failed to find relief anywhere else, turn to God to get rid of their miseries; they literally supplicate God to save their souls. Thus, to all these people God is an existential necessity. For a worshiper the particulars regarding the concept of God do not matter.

The ways of worship are also many. The simplest way is to worship in solitude with no external help. At the other end of the spectrum is collective worship when groups of people get together in some place of worship or in homes. Different religions have designated places of worship such as temples, churches, mosques etc. The form of worship also differs from person to person or religion to religion. Since it is not possible to see God and communicate with Him in person, all religions use symbolic actions during worship. They also use symbols to identify their faiths. All forms of worship are thus symbolic. Some people need to have a mental picture of God while worshiping. This picture may be just in their minds or they may need some physical object or image to represent God. Again this picture of God depends on the individual's faith. However, almost every religion sees God as omnipotent and omnipresent, i.e. He is all-powerful and is present everywhere.

The Hindu way of worship covers all the ways discussed above and the form of worship ranges from very simple to very elaborate. This is because Hinduism is very different from other religions; in fact it is not a religion in the traditional sense, it is a way of life. Unlike other major religions of the world Hinduism was not founded by any individual; it grew out of the accumulated spiritual experiences of innumerable sages (called *rishis* and *munis*) over a span of many centuries. It has almost no commandments (do this or don't do that) and in its purest form it has no dogmas. The concept of God and the universe is also different. He is still omnipotent and omnipresent but He is also all pervading, i.e. in everything. In fact the universe is not His creation but manifestation. At the beginning the universe grew out of Him and at the end it will dissolve into Him. God is infinite and we are all an infinitesimal part of Him. In that sense we are all a part of God. Through worship we try to elevate ourselves and make us worthy of merging with Him. When a person reaches that stage in life, he has become one with God. No other religion in the world has given man that much freedom — to say 'I am God'. This is one of the so-called great sentences in the scriptures. God is the ultimate reality, everything else is illusion and transitory. He is described as truth, consciousness, and bliss (*sat, chit, ānand*). God has no form, there are no physical qualities to describe Him, so He can not be seen, only realized. Since He has no form, He does not have a sex either; he can be thought of as male or female depending on an individual's perception.

This is the basic concept of God in Hinduism flowing from the philosophy expounded in the scriptures — the Vedās. While it is easy for sages and learned men to worship the abstract God, it is very difficult for the common man to worship without having a mental picture of God. And you can not form a mental picture of someone or something you have never seen. In order to bring the philosophy to the common man God had to be given a form. In relation to the man and the universe God has three main functions — creation, maintenance, and dissolution. These three aspects of God were represented by Brahmā, Vishnu and Mahesh, and the Hindu trinity was thus created. It is important to remember that we still have one God but three different representations.* Apart from the three aspects of God related to the task of running the universe, some people were enchanted with His power and wanted to worship that aspect separately. The Sanskrit word for power is *shakti* which is feminine. Now god was perceived as a woman. This did not present any contradiction, since He has no sex

---

*There is another aspect of the Trinity worth keeping in mind - the transition from formless (*nirākār*) to one having form (*sākār*). Brahmā is for all practical purposes without form. There are almost no temples devoted to him and there is no authentic picture depicting him, so he is still *nirākār*. Vishnu has a wide recognition in pictures and had two incarnations in human form. He may be considered totally *sākār*. We have temples of Vishnu as well as of Rāma and Krishna. *Shiva* has a well-depicted picture but he is enshrined in temples mostly in the form of *Shivalinga*. In villages this symbol is sometimes represented by a few smooth stones gathered from riverbeds. Thus Shiva is in the middle - both *nirākār* and *sākār*. Also, contrary to the popular notion that *Shivalinga* represents phallus, the origin of the term is related to the Vedic concept of the origin of the universe, according to which the first thing to appear was a golden egg floating in the infinite ocean. The dome like shape represents this golden egg and the basin below and around it symbolizes the ocean in the form of the water constantly being poured into it. The shape of the basin is made to allow the water to flow out. The word *linga* in Sanskrit means symbol; in this context originally it had nothing to do with human anatomy. That is why any smooth stone serves as the *Shivalinga* if a temple needs to be improvised.

to begin with; the idea of His male or female aspect was purely in the eyes of the worshiper. It was also not a new concept either. Even in the early *Vedic* period there is a reference to the female aspect of God*. Every type of power in the world can be put in one of three categories: intellectual, material (wealth and possessions), and physical. The female God was therefore represented by three goddesses — Saraswati, Laxmi and Pārvati. To bring it truly to the human level of understanding these three were paired with Brahmā, Vishnu and Mahesh respectively as their consorts. Since God is the creator and, hence, the ultimate father, it was natural to view the female aspect of God as the mother. Now there were six representations, each characterizing a particular aspect of just one God. Since there were no strict rules for the aspects of God to be worshipped, one was free to choose his own personal god. This led to a plethora of gods and goddesses and building of temples to enshrine them. To an outsider it may appear that Hinduism has a multitude of Gods but taking a closer look he would realize that all the gods and goddesses represent some partial aspect of the same one God. Again no other religion gives man the freedom to choose his own personal God. With freedom, of course, comes responsibility and a balance between the two is necessary in order to maintain a proper perspective.

Some people, especially children brought up outside India, have difficulty in understanding how one God can be different beings to different worshipers. In a way that sort of multiple role occurs in every day life. In a family a man is son to his parents, father to his children, husband to his wife, friend to other men and so on. Yet he is just one

* *Parāshakti devi sarvātmikā.* (all pervading energy). Rigveda I, 10-125. *Tvam stree tvam pumānasi* .. Svetāshwatar Upanishad, 4.1, 4.3.

individual. We do not have any problem in seeing him in diverse capacities. God can have different aspects of His existence in the same way and has the added advantage of not having any form or physical features to identify Him. The different facets of His existence are created by men depending on their own faith and conviction. In a purely abstract sense God is not a person whom we can approach, touch His feet, and pay respect. God is a state of existence, the highest one possible. If and when a person elevates himself to that level, he becomes one with God. That is what nirvāna is all about.

The artists among the worshipers sought to draw pictures of these gods and goddesses using their imagination but conforming to the original concept of God. Statues and idols were made from these pictures and installed in the temples where masses could go and worship. The philosophy is not for the masses, however; in order to bring the teaching of the scriptures to the common man another class of religious books *(purānas)* sought to teach the philosophy through stories that formed the bulk of Hindu mythology. These books were mostly devoted to one god or goddess and to some extent led to a sectarian division. The stories were narratives but the moral of the tales involved the philosophical points. Thus the plethora of gods and goddesses satisfied the needs of the masses but over time the main objective was generally lost sight of. Concurrent with the development of mythology were other attempts to bring the teachings of the *Vedas* to the masses. The most successful were the two epics — Rāmāyana and Mahābhārata, which attempted to condense the teachings of the scriptures in stories set in historical contexts. The epics dealt with two incarnations of God - Rāma and Krishna, who were quickly elevated to super-god status and enshrined in temples. Associated with the mythology and the epics were certain places, mountains and rivers which came to be regarded holy. Famous temples were built in these places and they became pilgrimage centers. Visits to these places and glimpses of the deities enshrined in them were thought as stepping stones for nirvāna.

Looking at the multitude of gods, an outsider might think that Hindus are idol worshipers. In medieval age a lot of destruction and carnage occurred because of this misconception. Even now some bigots think that way. We worship not the stone but the divinity which it is symbolic of. God is not made of stone or an image on paper. When we look at the photograph of a person, we spontaneously think or say who that is. But what we are looking at is a piece of paper and that person is certainly not made of paper. The photograph is simply a representation of that person at some place and time. Every religion uses symbols and symbolic gestures to convey certain ideas. The representation of different facets of God by idols and images is no different.

The basic concept of worship has not changed over the past several thousand years even though there has been a considerable degeneration of the religious order and system. The form of worship is still an individual choice. It is not necessary to go to a temple, you can make a temple at home or even in your heart. The external aspects are secondary. You can also worship collectively at home or in any other convenient place. The main requirement is having a proper atmosphere. People go to temples because these are supposed to have that proper atmosphere. In your house or somewhere else you have to create the atmosphere. Irrespective of where you worship there are certain norms and codes of conduct to be followed. To some these may seem meaningless rituals but a close examination will reveal their significance in the process of worship and, in some cases, their contribution to healthy body and mind.

CHAPTER TWO

TRADITIONS AND COMMONSENSE

When you go to a temple there are certain rules to be observed. The very first of them is to take off your shoes before entering the premises. This is true whether you go to a regular temple or one set up temporarily for a particular occasion. It is a sacred place where we go to worship and its sanctity must be respected. Keeping the place and the atmosphere clean is essential. Walking along streets the shoes pick up dirt and track the dirt to the inside of buildings. So taking off shoes outside of the temple is dictated by the need for cleanliness and hygiene. Some people also wash their hands and feet before entering the temple. This is not very different from the practice of taking a shower before saying your prayers at home. Worship is a spiritual act and has to be done in a clean place with clean body and mind. This practice of taking off shoes is followed also in traditional Hindu homes; the home in itself is a temple. Going to a regular temple may be an occasional or periodic affair; worship as a daily routine is always done at home. Religious ceremonies are performed at home and the personal God is always with you there.

Entering the temple one approaches the deity to pay homage. This is usually done by bowing the head before the image with joined palms, starting from the level of the heart and going to the forehead. This is also the traditional way of greeting elders and guests. A more humble way is to kneel down in front of the deity and put the forehead on the ground. There are some other variations of this approach such as lying prostate on the floor instead of kneeling. The idea is to show humility before God and realize that He is above everything. This is expressed also by putting the image on an elevated platform so that the deity literally sits higher than the devotees. As we shall see later, for a Hindu the daily life and religion are intertwined. So this practice of showing humility is not restricted to temple visits; once inculcated as a habit it becomes a part of daily life. Humility is the first step to greatness. In traditional families it is a common practice to bend and touch the feet of parents, grandparents, and other elderly persons. In the temple the priest or other functionaries generally perform the rituals of the worship, most people sit and observe. The floor is bare of furniture and they sit on the carpet with clean sheets spread over it. These motions that one goes through after entering the temple are not merely mechanical gestures. Besides showing humility they also benefit the physical health. Bowing the head and bringing it below the level of the heart makes it easier for the heart to pump blood to the head because the flow is aided by gravity. There are special exercises in yoga that accomplish this in a more elaborate way. Similarly bringing the palms together creates a special arrangement of the tiny electric and magnetic currents that are constantly flowing in the body. When the palms are joined, the current flow in the upper part of the body is modified and it benefits the head, lungs and heart. The body is a very complex electromagnetic system; any change in the position of various parts changes the current flow. This is one of the reasons why so many positions and postures are practiced in yoga. Finally, sitting on the floor is in itself an exercise. Since there is no external support available the person is forced to keep the back straight no matter what position he is in. Those who are in the habit of sitting on the floor for extended periods rarely have back problems.

The next phase of the temple visit involves the rituals. These rituals are symbolic and their significance goes far beyond the mechanical actions they appear to be. There is always a lighted lamp or set of lamps at the feet of the deity. Incense sticks burn constantly spreading their aroma. You may have wondered why we light a tiny lamp with *ghee* and cotton wick when there is plenty of light from the electric bulbs or tubes. After all, the light from the lamp is insignificant compared to the electric. To see the real meaning we have to understand the motive in the process of worship. In order to reach God one has to shed ignorance and acquire knowledge; in fact this is required for any progress even in day to day life. Darkness is associated with ignorance and light with knowledge. Lighting the lamp is a symbolic gesture that requests the deity to dispel our ignorance and to impart knowledge. It also represents our resolve to pursue that goal. The incense is kept burning to keep the air clean. It also has deodorant and disinfectant properties. With a large gathering in a relatively closed space the air has to be cleaned.

The other visible aspect of the worship is the offerings made to the deity. These are in the form of flowers, fruits, sweets or some other preparation made specifically for the occasion. Giving flowers to someone is a symbolic gesture of love and respect. Flowers are one of the most beautiful things in nature. Their life span is short, they bloom and then fade. In their short lives they bring beauty, grace, and serenity to the world. They are used on all occasions everywhere. It is a common practice to garland visiting dignitaries or distinguished guests. Women use them as ornaments, men use them to enhance elegance. Most flowers have fragrance emanating from them, which has a soothing effect. Flowers soothe not only our senses but also our hearts. Another aspect of flowers is that they are delicate and transitory. Even if they are not picked and used, they wither away in a short time. In the midst of all the beauty and grace they also remind us of the delicate nature of human relationships, including that with God, and of the fleeting time. When we offer flowers to the deity, we are not only giving Him back one of the best of His creations but also expressing our realization of the transitory nature of life and to use the present to the best of our ability. In nature fruits follow flowers, so we also offer fruits to the deity. After fruits we offer sweets in some form or other. Sweetness is associated with beauty, grace and innocence. The word sweet is used to denote that. We often hear of sweet songs, sweet voice, sweet child and so on. The concept of sweetness goes beyond the taste in the mouth. Even in the material sense sweets are used to mark happiness. The daily meals end with dessert. So it is only appropriate that we offer sweets to the deity during the worship.

At first glance this offering of fruits, sweets, or other eatables may seem ridiculous. We know that the deity enshrined in the temple can not eat. We sometimes do hear of a deity drinking milk or some ashes falling from the hands.

If it is true, it constitutes a miracle; otherwise it is sensational rumor mongering. The fact is that the image can not perform live functions. God can, because He is everywhere and conscious of everything. He has no form and can perform these actions unseen. It is this belief that makes the offerings *prasād* because He has tasted everything and now these are leftovers. Although the image is not God, it is a representation of some aspect of Him that we have chosen to worship. The very fact that we have chosen the image for that purpose, expresses our belief that God is actually present. To Him it does not matter what we offer. The offerings are an expression of our feelings and that is all that matters. We, our possessions — everything is His, we are just custodians. So we offer back His things to Him; in fact the prayer at the end of the worship says that. It is the feelings and the devotion that count. There are any number of stories in the Epics and *Purānas* to illustrate this point. In Rāmāyana there is a woman named Shabari belonging to one of the aboriginal tribes. She is a single-minded devotee of *Rāma* and is ecstatic to find that her idol is in the forest and would visit her. She can offer to Rāma only wild berries but she wants to be sure that they are very sweet. So while plucking the berries she tastes each one before putting in her basket. She offers the berries to *Rāma* who eats them with relish. In Mahābhārata Krishna once visited Vidur (step brother of Dhritrāshtra and Pāndu) who had only boiled green leaves (*sāg*) to offer. Krishna ate as if it were the most delicious preparation. In Shiva *Purāna* the most recommended offering to *Shiva* in the *Shivarātri* worship is leaf (*bilva-patra*) and water. There is a verse in Bhagavad Gita, in which Krishna says : "Whoever offers me with devotion a leaf, a flower, a fruit or even water, I accept that as a devout gift of the pure-minded". (*B.G.* 9.26).

The idea of viewing everything as God-given is expressed by families all over the world in the form of grace before meals. If a person has this belief all the time, he is always in the worship mode. It is important to realize that the words and feelings must match. Saying something without really meaning it is hypocrisy. This brings us to another item in collective worship. A considerable portion of the program is devoted to singing prayers or *bhajans*. In prayers we pray to God to give us something; it may be spiritual or material. Sometimes the prayers just praise God. *Bhajans* are a repetitive recitation of God's name. The word comes from the root *bhaj* that means repeating. In practice, though, *bhajans* are just songs describing God or His activities in various incarnations and may even include prayers. Most of these can be, and are, sung collectively. Singing *bhajans* is not a mechanical process. The singer must be conscious of the word meanings and the feelings inside must match the meaning. There is a famous prayer in Sanskrit recited quite often during worship, individual or collective. It addresses God : "You are mother, father, brother, friend; you are my knowledge as well as my possessions, in fact you are all and everything for me." If you are singing this verse but thinking of your family, bank account, or job, the action is simply mechanical.

The last item of the agenda is usually *ārati*. Special songs have been written for this purpose; some are universal addressing God, others are specifically for particular deities. *Ārati* itself consists of taking a lamp or number of lamps in one plate and moving it slowly in circles in front of the deity so that every part of the image is illuminated by the lamps. The light is reflected back to the lamps and symbolically it is thus supposed to have been graced by God. Also, by looking at the deity intently while doing *ārati* the image of

God is imprinted on the mind and heart of the devotee. Afterwards the plate is passed around and people partake of this blessing by putting their palms above the lamps and then touching their eyes and head. The origin of *ārati* is obscure but it must have become widespread with the proliferation of gods and temples. The term comes from the *Sanskrit* word *ārārtikā*; it's literal meaning is taking one's troubles and giving happiness and blessing in return; it also signifies respect and welcome. In that sense *ārati* is performed for the bridegroom coming for the marriage ceremony and also for distinguished visitors. Perhaps it originated from the age-old practice of parents, especially mothers, and elders expressing the sentiment of taking the child's troubles (in *Hindi* this practice is commonly known as *balaiān lenā*). A sense of deep love and devotion is behind this sentiment. In the case of God, however, it is hard to understand this concept. God is all-powerful. He is not supposed to have any troubles which the devotee can take on himself. In a philosophical sense, though, He is responsible for maintaining the creation in good order and upward progress. To that extent He has problems if people act in improper ways. By resolving to follow a path of spiritual uplift they are, in a way, taking away His troubles.

Singing is synonymous with music. In collective worship common musical instruments are used depending on the availability of the instruments as well as persons to play them. The music touches one's heart and soul. It creates an atmosphere when people lose themselves in the act of listening. It is not uncommon to see people listening to music make spontaneous gestures with their hands and heads without realizing it. For the active participants it may lead to ecstasy when they are in a trance and unaware of anything except what their mind is fixed on. In that sense the music promotes concentration. Also there is an intimate connection between spoken word and thought; the voice is simply an expression of the thought. But this relationship can be sometimes reversed. Repeated chanting of words can awaken corresponding thoughts in the mind. For most people the second process is easier and that is why the chanting of mantras or God's name has been given prominence in worship. If only God's name is recited repeatedly it is called *japa*, while a collection of mantras describing the attributes of God is called *stotra* which is another word for prayer. During the worship the thought and.words must go together*. Otherwise there is no sincerity and, hence, no devotion and the worship becomes a mechanical and meaningless exercise.

So far we have discussed only collective worship because most people worship that way. But worship can take any form and some people prefer to do it individually. The individual has his own concept of God and worships accordingly. It may be the same as in collective worship or totally different. There are many ways to approach God. The collective worship follows the path of devotion. Here one devotes himself completely to God. He considers all his actions as following God's will. He does not read scriptures to acquire knowledge. Knowing God is the ultimate

---

* There is an interesting anecdote in *Shatpath Brāhmaṇa* which is from *Shukla Yajurveda*. Once an altercation arose between Speech (*Vāk*) and Mind (*Man*) as to who had the greater importance. They could not settle the issue and went to Brahmā for arbitration. After listening to both sides Brahmā decided that Mind had superiority over Speech because the latter only articulated what the former conceived of. Speech got angry with Brahmā and vowed not to have anything to do with him. That is why during yajnas the offerings to Brahmā are made silently - the mantras are not chanted.

knowledge and he hopes to get that through devotion. At the other end is the path of knowledge. Here the external aspects of worship are absent. As stated earlier, all those actions are symbolic. The person following the path of knowledge knows the real objective and has no need for symbols. He tries to understand the nature of God and his relationship with Him; once he reaches the stage where he knows God, he has reached the goal. But he also realizes that the path itself is the goal, since there is no end to acquiring knowledge. This is very tersely expressed in the Upanishadas in the form of the question : "How can the knower be known ?"* Ultimately God has to be realized, not known, and realizing God is a matter of experience not investigation. In between these two paths is the path of action which most people follow. The essence of this approach is that one should do his normal duties sincerely and without selfish motives. He should consider all his actions as God's. The individual worshiper can follow any of these paths. If he understands the philosophy, he does not need any image or deity. His heart is the temple and God is enshrined there.

★ ★ ★

---

* *Vigyātāram are ken vijāneeyāt* - Brihad. Up. 2-4-14

CHAPTER THREE

RELIGION AND FAITH

Religion is usually defined as an organized system of beliefs and rituals centering on supernatural being(s). Sometimes faith is used in the same sense as religion because faith essentially means believing in something. However, faith is a more general term and may not have anything to do with religion. For example, one can have faith in parents, friends, or in oneself without belonging to any religion. If one has faith in God, he is supposed to be religious. But the existence of God is not necessary for some religions. For example, Buddha did not believe that there is a God, at least not in the same sense as others did. It is ironical that later on his followers elevated him to the level of God. The concept of God and His relationship with man is different in different religions. This brings us to the question : Did man create God? And considering all the problems that the religious differences have created in the world, it is not a superfluous question. All religions believe that God created the universe. So there is only one God that all religions worship. However, the masses following a particular religion begin to think their God as the only one, not realizing that the difference is only in the way of approaching God. This way of thinking evolves from blind faith and leads to a narrow view of God and man's interaction with Him that results in conflicts. The ideal situation will be if there was only one religion. There have been several movements to achieve this goal but with little success. So even if man did not invent God, he has created varying concepts that have led to combative attitudes and frequent conflicts.

Every religion adopts a moral code that, in some cases, leads to a set of strict rules of behavior that become a distinguishing mark of that religion. Often these rules have little to do with the philosophical core of the religion. The basic aim of any religion is to help man to uplift himself and approach God. This leads to the need for realizing the distinction between good and evil, right and wrong. The moral code defines these terms and to that extent these distinctions are man made. Although there are certain areas of behavior where these definitions are common, in many cases differences arise. What is right in one religion is not necessarily so in others. For example, killing or hurting any living being is considered wrong in almost all religions. But in meat eating societies killing animals for food is an accepted norm and, therefore, it is right. Thus right and wrong are not always self-evident. The same is true for good and evil. When a religion is based on a philosophy and the code has been developed on the basis of accumulated experience, the accepted definitions of these opposites are more likely to be closer to universal. Within certain general guidelines the individual has a right to decide for himself based on his own convictions. And this is what the worship of God is supposed to do to a person — to guide him to a righteous path. Hinduism is one such religion; the actual name is *sanātan dharma*, i.e. eternal religion and comes closest to the concept of universal religion. Buddhism, Jainism, and Sikhism are simply its offshoots. It may be worthwhile to mention also *Ārya Samāj*; it is not an offshoot but goes back to the abstract concept of God without form and specific qualities. Unlike the traditional *sanātan dharma* it does not subscribe to the idea and worship of God in form of idols.

Religion is a part of life and it can not be separated from daily life. The religious activity does not end with worship in temple or church or mosque. It is reflected in every action. In Hinduism religion becomes a part of life at birth and remains so until death or even beyond. God is everywhere and watches all our activities. If we think that by building churches, temples, and mosques we have confined God in a narrow space and we need to be conscious of His presence only while visiting these places, we are not religious. The idea that we can do anything away from the place of worship and get it washed out by praying to God in the confines of these sacred places, is contrary to any religious belief. We can not do anything behind Gods back, He has no back.

Another concept common to every religion is that of heaven and hell. Heaven is supposed to be the abode of God, angels, and souls granted salvation. Hell is the abode of devils and wicked souls sent there after death for punishment. These are almost literal meanings corresponding to the beliefs of general masses. In a more general sense heaven is the place or state of great happiness or bliss; hell is a place or situation of evil and misery. Again the details and graphical description of heaven and hell differ from religion to religion. In this case we can reasonably say that these concepts were created by man and this is a classic example of the carrot and stick used by religions to keep people straight. The element of fear keeps man from straying and the aspiration to reach heaven makes him strive to be worthy of the place. Is there a life after death? In most religions the answer is yes but the concepts are different. The simplest and perhaps the most common is the belief that after death the person goes either to heaven or to hell, although there is a possibility that he may exist on earth as ghost. In Hinduism the idea of heaven as the abode of gods has existed from the beginning and was reinforced with the proliferation of gods. However, it was not the abode of God. Every soul is a tiny part of the infinite God. Birth and death make up a cycle of existence of the soul on earth, i.e. one who dies gets born again and one who is born is sure to die. This is the so-called theory of rebirth. The soul carries the imprint of all actions good or bad, performed by a person. When good actions wash away the bad ones, the soul is pure and returns to the infinite. This is what we call salvation or nirvana. As we saw earlier, in its abstract form the concept of God is a state of existence and in that context we may think of heaven as the state of bliss. Hell was introduced much later when *puranas* were written for the masses. The stories in these do use the element of fear to keep men on the religious path. Those who follow the path of knowledge to reach God do not think of heaven or hell. However, heaven and hell do not exist only in the mind; they exist right here on earth in the form of extremes of happiness and misery. What happens after death is either philosophy or speculation but what happens during one's life in this world is real. The worship of and the faith in God help one to make life better right here. The fruits of worship remain with the person in the life after death.

CHAPTER FOUR

THE OTHER SIDE OF THE COIN

Faith is an essential ingredient of religious life. However, even faith has to be rational; blind faith, even in God, can be disastrous. The purpose of worship and religious living is to give the person inner strength to cope with the problems of life in whatever form they may come. It is through the person himself that God provides the help. To expect that He will help as an external force is to shirk one's own responsibility. History has taught us that this was one degeneration in Hindu attitude that plunged the society into despair. Too much reliance on God's intervention at times of danger led to ruin and carnage. While the temples were being demolished and people massacred, faith in God (*bhakti*) required physical resistance to aggression and not passive imploring in the front of the deity. People lost sight of the basic idea that God was in every one of them and He could act only through them. *Bhakti* should be an expression of inner strength and not of despair, it should lead to activity, not passivity. There seems to have been a widespread misconception of the term 'complete surrender to the Lord,' especially among the adherents of the *bhakti marg*. They quote numerous verses from Gitā (18-66, for example) to justify the attitude that all problems in life would be taken care of by worshipping God. Complete surrender refers to mental attitude and not physical activity. God can not perform any action, He does things through the people. A person who is acting according to his inner conviction is doing God's bidding. To surrender to God one does not have to sit in front of the image all the time, he carries the image in his heart wherever he goes. In our propensity for transcendental pursuits we should not lose sight of the fact that the world, as long as we live in it, is real and the present can not be ignored in preparation for the future. The path of devotion and that of action need not be separate.

Taking the words from the scriptures literally can also create problems. For example, in Gitā the Lord says that whenever there is a serious decline in *dharmā* (righteousness) and rise of *adharma* (unrighteousness) in this world, He incarnates in human form to protect the righteous and punish the wicked, and thus restore order (4. 7-8). While we do not doubt the Lord's words, the intent here is that when things get bad, people having faith in Him and themselves will rise to the occasion and the society will produce a leader who will fulfil His promise. If people do nothing except implore Him to perform miracles, nothing will happen. There is a lot of truth to the saying that God helps those who help themselves.

The Caste System

There is one dark side of Hindu society - the caste system that is always cited as a negative point. It is necessary to make it clear right at the start that the caste system prevalent in the society for the past several centuries is not a part of the religion. The caste system had been originally devised as a division of labor and had nothing to do with the parentage of the person. There are any number of examples in the scriptures and the Epics to illustrate that a person's worth was judged by his knowledge and actions and not by his birth. With time people in influential positions in the society exploited the system and it degenerated into a despicable practice. The intellectuals and free thinkers of the society felt disgusted and rebelled against such practices. Reformist groups appeared as early as the seventh century BC and several groups sprang up to spearhead the movement. Some of them questioned not only the practices but also the basic tenets of the vedic teachings and bordered on being agnostics or even atheists. Two that gained prominence and proved enduring were Jains and Buddhists. The caste system became almost extinct for a short period during the hey-days of Buddhism but regained its foothold after Buddhism itself became almost extinct in India. With the Muslim domination and political fragmentation of the country the caste system became a firmly rooted institution. Even with the consolidation of the country in the latter half of the nineteenth century, the British maintained a hands-off attitude in this matter. In the past hundred years, though, a number of reform movements sprang up to correct the wrongs and made remarkable progress in alleviating the situation. At present the caste system is almost nonexistent in urban areas and among educated public. Every society and culture goes through some unpleasant experiences. The serfdom and slavery in the western societies were not laudable either. The important point is that the society recognizes and tries to correct the problem.

PART TWO

PART TWO

CHAPTER ONE

RELIGIOUS RITES

Rituals and symbolism are essential features of every religion. Rituals are generally prescribed in some religious texts and are a set of rules that govern the sequence of performing worship or ceremonies. In Hinduism all rituals start with purification of the person as well as of the place. Water is symbolic of purification as it is used in day to day life for bathing, washing, etc. Therefore all the rituals use water as the starting element. For worship a person must have clean body and mind; the place where he worships must be clean. So the first thing one starts with is personal purification. One takes a little water in his hand and while chanting the special mantra for this ritual he sprinkles the water all over his body. The mantra simply states that whatever the state the person is in, with the grace of God he is purified both outside and inside. The next step is to pray for all the parts of the body to function efficiently. For this purpose he again takes a little water in his left hand and dipping his fingers of the right hand he touches his mouth, nose, eyes, arms and thighs while reciting the mantra for this step. Next comes the purification of the place. Again while reciting the appropriate mantra he sprinkles water over the place where the worship is to be done. These are all symbolic gestures. The people performing the rites and even those participating in the function have already taken showers and the place has already been thoroughly cleaned. The rites are not for purification in the physical sense but for ensuring that everyone concerned understands the need and significance of maintaining clean body and surroundings. Touching of the body parts signifies a resolve to be physically fit, realizing that good health is essential for good life and that it can not happen without the grace of God. After this the rituals are specific for specific worship. In general the particular deity or deities are invoked and requested to grace the occasion and they are worshipped individually or collectively. Here we have to remind ourselves that we are worshiping different aspects of God and the number of deities can be whatever we choose.

In the early stages of the development of the religion people worshiped nature as manifestation of God and the gods mostly represented the elements of nature. The prominent ones were — fire god (*Agni*), water god (*Varuna*), and air god (*Vāyu*) because they are essential for life to exist. Later these elements retained their special place in all forms of worship. Fire occupied a special place right from the beginning and was used in every ritual. Fire produces light and light symbolizes knowledge. It is by light that we see things and therefore fire sees everything. Therefore it came to be regarded as the ultimate witness. It also consumes everything, so it became the principal element in *yajna* for making offerings to all gods. The act of offering is called *havan* or *hom* and these are an essential part of almost all important ceremonies. Many people, especially those following *Ārya Samāj* branch, perform *havan* by itself instead of as a part of formal worship of any deity. The process starts with the usual purification steps. The fire is then started with the chanting of a special mantra and the offering is in the form of *ghee* (clarified butter) and a specially prepared mixture of herbs. The practice started in the early days for propitiating the gods but it has some practical significance as well. The *ghee* is highly flammable like oil and it keeps the flame strong. As it burns it also produces a special aroma and so does the special mixture. The process thus acts as air freshener. The first offering is to fire itself and the subsequent ones are to different gods. The initial offerings are common to all *homs*; after that there are different *homs* for different ceremonies. Each offering is done with a mantra; the first part of the mantra simply means that we offer all we have to the particular god, the second part says it is that god's, not mine. The mixture and *ghee* represent our possessions. This is a sentiment that permeates through truly religious people all over the world; whatever we have is due to the grace of God and therefore it is His. The first part of the mantra ends with the word *svāhā* and the offering into the fire is made with this word.

Sometimes *havan* is performed on a much larger scale and it is called *yajna*. This is generally a community affair and lasts much longer than the usual *havan* done in homes or temples. In ancient times the learning centers were associated with prominent sages and the students as a group performed *yajna* as a daily routine. A place was permanently reserved for performing *yajna* and the fire was never allowed to go out. Although as a ceremony *yajnas* were performed to propitiate God, there is a deep philosophy behind the process. The external aspect is just a symbolic representation. Life itself is *yajna*, the fire burning within us sustains life. Whatever we eat and drink is an offering to this fire. This is the physical aspect. On the spiritual side every action of man is an offering to God and, therefore, the action constitutes *yajna*. If a person does everything as a will of God and dedicates every action to Him, he is performing *yajna* all the time. With this knowledge he does not have to engage in the symbolic rituals. However, those who have not reached that spiritual level, perform the rituals in order to get the knowledge. This was the idea behind the collective *yajnas* performed by students under the guidance of their guru. There is another aspect of collective *havans* that needs mention. These are performed on some auspicious day determined from the special calendar. This is also true for worships and ceremonies, although Hindus outside India have to make some adjustments because of practical considerations. Hindu astrology is based on the configuration of the planets and stars and the auspicious nature of a moment or a day depends on this configuration and the phase of the moon. It is very interesting to note that the predictions about eclipses made on the basis of astrology coincide exactly with those made by modern astronomy. In fact, the estimates of the age of universe given in the scriptures thousands of years ago are remarkably close to those provided by modern astrophysics.

CHAPTER TWO

CEREMONIES

In Hinduism religion is an inseparable part of life and remains with a person from beginning to the end. According to Hindu belief life begins at conception. Even until the last century the birth date of a person was taken to be the date of conception, which was easy to determine if the steps prescribed in the scriptures were followed. There are a total of sixteen ceremonies prescribed during the life span; these are called *samskārs*. The first one is the ceremony for conception, the last one is the ceremony for funeral. Those in between mark the different stages of the child and adult life. Two of these ceremonies come before the birth of the child and are performed to wish for and ensure a healthy development of the child growing inside the mother's womb. The next ceremony is at birth and is essentially a way of expressing gratitude to God and praying for a healthy and fruitful life of the child. After this comes the naming ceremony. In India naming the child just after birth is not obligatory even for those born in hospitals. The naming ceremony is performed anytime after eleven days from birth but before the child's first birthday. When the child is a few weeks old a ceremony is performed for taking him out of the house for the first time. As he grows and is ready to take food other than mother's milk, a ceremony is performed to give him food for the first time. Then comes the ceremony for the first haircut; this is usually done at the age of three to five. Traditionally the child gets a clean shave to get rid of the hair he was born with. This promotes a profuse and healthy growth of hair. The next ceremony is that of ear piercing which was obligatory for girls but in some communities it was done for boys as well. When boys reached adolescence they had the sacred thread (*upanayan*) ceremony. This is the only ceremony which is exclusively for boys. This marked the beginning of their formal education and in ancient times they went away to live with their gurus for a prolonged period. There were other ceremonies performed during the study period but the next significant one was the return after completion of the studies. The most important one came after that - the marriage ceremony. Thereafter the ceremonies were performed to mark the different stages in life. According to the Hindu philosophy there are four main stages of life - *brahmacharya* covering childhood and adolescence, *grihastha* starting from the marriage and lasting until all children are grown up and self-supporting, *vānprastha* extending up to retirement, and *sanyās* for the rest of the life. The last ceremony is, of course, the funeral or the last rites. Very few families, if any, perform all of the prescribed ceremonies. Almost all families perform the marriage and the last rites. Most traditional families perform the sacred thread ceremony; in some parts of India its importance is on par with marriage and last rites. The birth and first haircut ceremonies are popular even outside India. We will limit ourselves to the discussion of the three main ones.

The procedures and mantras for these ceremonies are given in a special group of scriptures called *sutrās*. Most of the *mantras* used in the ceremonies come from two *vedās* – - *Rig* and *Yajur*. We will talk about the Vedās and scriptures later but it is necessary to state here that these are all in Sanskrit, from which Hindi and most of the regional languages in India are derived. The general public does not have a working knowledge of Sanskrit and the generation born and growing up outside India have little exposure to that language. One may reasonably ask why the ceremonies have to be done in a language that very few can understand. As originally intended, the mantras if chanted with proper pronunciation and stresses produce a solemn atmosphere in which the ceremony has to be performed. They also provide a spiritual link to God who is invoked to witness and bless the ceremony. For example, if a singer were just to read the song, it would hardly produce the same effect as singing in proper rhythm. Or if he sings without the accompanying music, the atmosphere created would not be the same. If a number of instruments are being played simultaneously as in an orchestra, they have to be properly coordinated through a composition. The chanting of the mantras and the feelings of the performer must also be coordinated in order to have the desired effect. There are strict rules for chanting mantras and just as in music, simply reading them or providing translation in another language will not do. Everyone listening to classical music does not understand the intricacies of the composition but enjoys all the same. He is transported into the atmosphere created by the music, which is not a physical but spiritual experience. If a person attending the ceremony participates with his whole being, he would experience the same spiritual bond. As a language

Sanskrit is not difficult to learn. Apart from the scriptures it has a rich literature. There are some short-term intensive courses that provide the ability to carry on simple conversations. An added advantage of knowing Sanskrit is that it makes learning some other foreign languages such as Russian much easier because of some similarities in grammar and syntax.

Sacred Thread Ceremony

This ceremony, called *upanayan,* marks the beginning of adolescence and the start of formal education. In ancient times there were no formal schools and boys received their education at the feet of the gurus who were prominent and revered sages. Later on many prominent educational centers developed more or less on the pattern of the modern universities. Some like Nālandā and Taxshilā became internationally famous. But these institutions retained the tradition of guru and disciple of the sage era. The word *upanayan* has two syllables — *upa* meaning near and *nayan* meaning to approach. Thus *upanayan* means to go near and literally it meant to go to the guru. Traditionally guru is to be regarded as embodiment of God and in that sense the word also means going to God. The purpose of the ceremony was to get the boy emotionally ready for the new phase of life. The ritual starts with the usual purification steps, starting the fire for *havan*, and the boy wears the sacred thread with silent chanting of *Gāyatri* mantra. The sacred thread (called *yajnopaveet*) consists of three strands tied at the ends in a special knot thus forming a closed loop; the length of the strands is about five feet. It goes over the left shoulder and around the head and right arm so that the top part is on the left shoulder and the bottom is a little below the waist on the right side. The three threads are meant to constantly remind the person of his three debts to parents, society, and God. They also signify his resolve to pursue the goals of physical, material and spiritual prosperity. Yet another interpretation is that the three individual threads represent the Trinity — Brahmā, Vishṇu and Mahesh and the knot expresses the fact that the three are only three different aspects of one God. The sacred thread is not supposed to part the body during lifetime except for replacement, when the new one is put on while the old one slides down the body. There are a few other rituals that are performed after the boy gets the sacred thread. The boy is given a stick and a pot for collecting food. Then he goes around asking for alms from parents and other elders assembled for the occasion. This is symbolic and remnant of the practice in ancient times when the students used to go around and collect food from the neighborhood and bring back to the guru for collective meals. In the present conditions its significance lies in the realization that even in his student days, the boy should try to do something constructive for himself as well as for the society.

Here again we get into the controversial aspect of the caste system. According to the *sutrās* this ceremony is prescribed only for the three upper castes, the lower one is not entitled to get the sacred thread. But we need to go back to the original concept of the caste system when the caste was determined by the work one performs. There is a story in Mahābhārata, in which Yudhishthir was asked some questions by a celestial being (*Yaksha*) and the life of his brothers depended on satisfactory answers. One of the questions was : How does a person become Brāhmin, by birth, education, or action? In reply Yudhishthir said : "A man does not become Brāhmin by birth or education, he becomes that only by his actions." This is what the early sages had intended but with time the system degenerated.

However, with gradual eradication of the system we may again get back to the original basis of division of labor.

Marriage Ceremony

Marriage is probably the most significant of the ceremonies largely because it is also a well-attended social event. In the individual's life it is certainly a unique stage, since at this time two lives merge into one. That is the central point of the ceremony from a religious perspective. It marks the beginning of the second phase of life as a householder. Its spiritual and religious significance is far greater than that of the other ceremonies because it involves two bodies and souls. In Hinduism no external authority pronounces the couple husband and wife; they do it themselves with fire being the ultimate witness. The priest is there only to supervise and guide the ceremony. It is true that in most cases the priest chants the mantras but that happens simply because most brides and grooms are not well versed in Sanskrit. Otherwise they are required to chant the mantras themselves. In the programs printed and distributed on the occasion the title usually says Vedic wedding ceremony or something like that. All the ceremonies in Hinduism are Vedic; as stated earlier, these are prescribed in the scriptures and the mantras usually come from the two principal Vedas.

The ceremony usually starts with a welcome of the bridegroom and party by the family and friends of the bride. It is customary to honor the groom with *ārati* performed by an elder sister or another female member of the bride's family. The bride then garlands the groom and he in turn garlands the bride. These parts of the ceremony are traditional customs and have nothing to do with the religious aspect. After the usual purification rituals the main ceremony starts with the bride's parents offering the groom a seat and worshiping him. Then the parents give away the bride by offering her hand into the groom's hand and he accepts and holds her hand. The bride gets seated on the right side of the groom. The fire is started for *havan* and there are sixteen *homs* prescribed for the full ceremony, of which four are essential. In order to cut short the time only four are performed in most cases, at least outside India; with the full course of *havans* the ceremony lasts for several hours. The offerings into the fire are made by the bride and the groom. During the last *hom* the bride and groom walk around the fire (keeping it on their right) after each offering. The offering for this *hom* is different, it consists of puffed rice (actually puffed paddy called *lājā*). There are four rounds in all, in the first three the bride leads, the groom leads in the last. The number of rounds denotes the four objectives in life — religious, physical and material prosperity and finally salvation or nirvana. Before starting each round the bride, assisted by the groom, puts her right foot on a small stone. This signifies the resolve of the couple to go through together in good as well as bad times; walking on the stone symbolizes hard times. In the next part of the ceremony called *saptapadi,* the couple takes seven steps together signifying their mutual promise to be together in life. There is a separate mantra for taking each step. At each step the couple pray to God respectively for food, physical fitness, riches, happiness, possessions, seasonal goods, and finally, mutual love. In some parts of India, especially in the north, it became a custom to combine the two parts into one and seven rounds of the fire are made. It is hard to determine when and how it started but it is not in accord with the prescribed rites. After *saptapadi* the bridegroom puts his arm over the bride's shoulder touching her heart and both are supposed to repeat a special mantra. Through this mantra they promise to God and to each other that from now on their hearts and souls are united and though physically two bodies, they are spiritually one. Next the groom puts vermilion in the parting of the bride's hair. In some parts of India, especially in the south, the groom puts a special necklace (called *mangalsutra*) instead of putting the vermilion mark. After this the bride moves over to the left of the groom completing the process of becoming the left or better half of her husband. This completes the ceremony and the couple is blessed by all present.

Last Rites

This is the closing chapter in the life of an individual and the last ceremony for him. It is important to note that in the first and the last of the sixteen ceremonies the person himself does not participate. In the conception ceremony he has no physical existence as yet, in the last the fire has gone out of the body that has to be given back to fire. It is the soul and not the physical body that represents the person. The body is mainly the vehicle for the soul, although it has to be taken care of for the sake of the occupant. This symbolism goes back to the central belief in Hinduism — the soul is indestructible, it does not die. It came from the invisible into the body at conception and went back to the invisible after death. It goes through the cycle of birth and death until the actions in the life spans purify it, when it merges into the infinite. This is nirvana. What happens to the person after death depends on his actions during his lifetime. The soul carries the imprint of these actions which are cumulative. The action itself can not be undone, only its effect can be neutralized by another action. The last rites at the funeral are, therefore, for the benefit of the departed soul. The children of the person perform these. Depending on the place and circumstances, the body is taken to a clean open place or to a crematorium where the rituals are performed before the body is burned. The spot where the body is placed, is washed and cleaned and the body is placed there with the feet facing south. This is a tradition with its origin in mythology and may have some remote symbolism. The fire is lighted and offerings are made with appropriate mantras most of which are special for this occasion. One of the children, usually the eldest son, performs the rituals. After the offerings the son takes a piece of wood from the fire and goes around the body keeping it on his left. If the body is being burned in an open ground, he lights the pyre near the mouth after going around; if the rites are performed in a crematorium, he symbolically puts the burning end of the wood at the mouth. Then the body is put into the incinerator along with the fire. If the cremation is done in an open place the relatives usually wait until the body is completely consumed by the fire. The ashes are collected the next day and there is a ritual for that also. The ashes are then dispersed into the running water of a river. Thereafter special rituals are performed daily for eleven days and the rites end with family and relatives getting together for a collective dinner in the memory of the departed.

PART THREE

PART THREE

CHAPTER ONE

POPULAR POOJĀS

It is a common practice in Hindu families to have worship
on special occasions that also serve as social gatherings. The
common word for worship is *poojā* and there are some
poojās that are more popular than others. These may be
performed to celebrate some special occasion in the family,
to satisfy the spiritual aspirations, or to express gratitude to
God. The rituals are basically the same in all with some
variations in the details depending on the particular deity
being worshipped. The regional preferences and customs
also determine the popularity. These popular *poojās* are
almost invariably related to mythology and stories from
Purānas or the Epics. The narration of these stories becomes
the main part of the worship. As already mentioned, the
Purānas were written to convey the teachings of Vedās to
the common man through stories. Therefore these stories
have two facets to them, the narrative itself and the
philosophy behind it. If one can believe the story literally,
there is no problem. For others who find the narrative

intellectually unacceptable, it is necessary to delve into the philosophy. We are faced with the same problem as in the case of multitude of gods and goddesses representing one God. We will try to discuss briefly both facets of the stories.

Satyanārāyana Kathā : The word *Kathā* means story and this is a very popular form of collective worship in north and central parts of India. In some parts the word *Kathā* by itself is used for this *poojā*. The story is taken from *Skanda Purāna* and covers five chapters. It is narrated in original and translated into Hindi or the pertinent regional language for the benefit of the general audience. *Satyanārāyana* is simply another name of God (more specifically, of Vishnu) and the story illustrates the point that anyone can propitiate God by simple devotion irrespective of his position in the society. This story is narrated in greater detail in 'Appendix B' giving the narrative as well as its philosophical content.

Ganesha Poojā : In the hierarchy of the gods who appear in mythology, Ganesha has a special place. In all traditional ceremonies he is the first god to be invoked and worshiped. And the origin of this practice goes back to his own origin. He is literally a second-generation god being the second son of Shiva and Pārvati. The story of his birth is interesting. After their marriage Shiva and Pārvati made their household on Mount Kailāsh. Shiva was a wanderer by nature coming into and going out of the house as and when he pleased. This irked Pārvati as his habits were encroaching on her privacy. The household servants would not obey her when it came to restricting Shiva's movements. One day she decided to create her own personal guard who would obey only her. In those days women rubbed their bodies with herbal paste before taking bath. Usually the flakes left over after this operation were discarded but on this day she collected a large amount and created a son — a healthy handsome boy out of it. We recall that God created the universe by sheer will power so the various gods and goddesses could also do that. She gave a staff to him and placed him as a guard at the house entrance instructing him not to let anyone in while she was taking a bath inside. After a little while Shiva came back and tried to enter the house ignoring him but the boy blocked his way. Shiva asked :

"Who are you?"

"I am the son of mother Pārvati and she has instructed me not to let anyone in while she is taking a bath."

"Get out of my way boy!" shouted Shiva and tried to push past him.

But the boy turned out to have enormous strength and kept him at bay. Shiva got very angry, hurled his trident, and cut off the boy's head. Pārvati was just finishing her bath.

"How did you get in? I had told my guard not to let any one in."

"I cut his head off", he said off-handedly; he was still annoyed.

Pārvati started crying and would not stop. Then she got angry telling him to restore the boy to life or else... "

"Alright, I will do it."

While this was going on inside the house some mountain creature took off with the severed head. Shiva ordered his servants (*ganas*) to go out and bring the head of any young one sleeping away from his mother. In his agitated state he was not very specific. The *ganas* went out and after sometime they came back with a baby elephant's head. Shiva put the head on the lifeless body of the boy and brought him to life. Pārvati was still crying inside when he called her to show his proud achievement. At the strange sight of the boy with an elephant's head, she started crying more loudly.

"What have you done, what will be the fate of my son in this world ?"

"Don't you worry, he will be the lord of all these *ganas* and we will call him Ganesha. Hereafter he will be worshiped first in every ceremony." Up to this day when starting something people often say - let us do *Shri Ganesh*.

Thus was born Ganesha. The actual story in Ganesh Purāna is much longer with lot more details. Do we believe that a human form like Ganesha ever existed? It all depends on how an individual feels. If one can believe the story literally, it is fine. If not, we have to see the symbolism behind it. As we discussed earlier, God is one and the apparent multiplicity is attributable to the freedom to choose a personal god. God has no form but if we choose, He can have any form. Let us now look at the philosophy behind the story. The union of Shiva and Pārvati symbolizes the union of the finite soul with the infinite. This union can not take place as long as there is attachment with the world and material things. All the material bonds have to be cut off in order to reach God. The boy, made out of the discarded flakes, represents the material bondage. The material possessions have no value to the soul, they are always left behind. The severing of the boy's head symbolically represents the cutting off of the bondage. We then come to the elephant head. In the ages past the elephant was seen as a sign of wealth. The elephant is also supposed to be very intelligent, has keen eyesight and an acute distinguishing faculty; it can pick out a needle from a haystack. It is the only animal that drinks water in two stages, first it takes the water in the trunk and then puts it into the mouth. In order to be successful and prosperous in life one must have intelligence and the capacity to distinguish between good and bad. The combination of human body and elephant head represents the fulfillment of that requirement. This is also why Ganesh is regarded as the god of achievement and wealth.

Devi Jāgaran : Another form of popular *poojā*, especially in the northwest regions of India, is *Devi Jāgaran*. The word *Devi* literally means goddess and covers all aspects of the power of God and hence all the three principal goddesses. In this context, though, it refers to Pārvati and the *poojā* involves worshipping her through the night foregoing sleep, i.e. keeping awake all night. That is why it is called *Jāgaran* (keeping awake). The *poojā* starts with worship of Ganesha, then of Shiva before getting to the main deity. It is customary to read the story of the birth of Ganesha, chant prayers to Shiva, and read or chant the story from *Devi Mahātmya* (also called Durgā *Saptashati*), which describes the achievements of *Pārvati*. This book is a part of *Mārkandeya Purāna* and is the favorite of the devotees worshiping God as the Mother. The chanting and rituals are interspersed with popular *bhajans*. The worship ends at dawn with *ārati*.

Rāmāyana *Pāth* : Rāmāyana is one of the two main Epics in Hinduism. The object of the Epics was to summarize the teachings of the Vedās and Purānas in the form of stories revolving around the two most popular incarnations of Vishnu. Rāmāyana deals with the life of Rāma and was written by the great sage Vālmīki in Sanskrit. Subsequently, the same story was written in Hindi and other regional languages. The Hindi version was written by Tulsidās. Although the exact title of the book is Rāma Charit Mānas, it is popularly known as *Rāmāyana* in most parts of India.

The story in all versions is essentially the same. The main difference between Vālmīki's Rāmāyana and Tulsi's Mānas is the author's perspective. Vālmīki portrays Rāma as an ideal man and is not averse to showing his human flaws, while Tulsi sees him as embodiment of God incapable of having imperfections. In any case, Tulsi's Rāmāyana is popular with the masses and a very popular form of collective *poojā* is reading of Rāmāyana. This is done in two ways depending on the availability of time. The longer version of this *poojā* involves reading the entire book without any interruption. This takes about twenty-four hours. Most of the time several persons read simultaneously. When only one person is reading, as it happens at night, the changeover is done in such a way that the continuity is maintained. This is why the *Poojā* is called *Akhand* Rāmāyana *Pāth*, i.e. uninterrupted reading of Rāmāyana. The shorter version involves reading only a selected part of the book. The choice depends on the host family but the most favorite is *Sunder Kānd*, the part dealing with the exploits of Hanumān, also referred to as the monkey god particularly in the West. *Tulsi* portrays everyone associated with Rāma as an ideal. Hanumān is the ideal devotee serving the Lord without any reservations.

The *poojā* starts with the usual rituals of purification and invocation of gods. Then Vishnu is worshiped followed by the worship of Rāma as his incarnation. The reading starts at this point and continues until the book is finished. After the reading others participate in singing *bhajans*. The *Poojā* closes with *ārati* for Rāmāyana. This is the only occasion where *ārati* is performed for a book and not for a given deity, even though in a general sense it represents *ārati* for Rāma and everyone associated with him.

Gitā Pāth : Some people take a slightly different *Path* for *poojā* by reading from the scriptures. They may prefer to follow the *Path* of knowledge instead of that of devotion. They may read verses from Upanishads. As we shall discuss later, Upanishads are the philosophical parts of the *Vedās* and they form the basis of Hinduism. Bhagavad Gitā (popularly called just Gitā) is a part of the other Epic, Mahābhārata; it summarizes the philosophy of Vedās blending it with ideas from another school of philosophy called *Sānkhya*. In course of time this part was placed as an independent book and came to be regarded on par with Upanishads. It is a relatively short book and takes two to three hours for reading from beginning to end. Some learned individual may explain the meaning to the audience as he goes along. In this case only one or two of the eighteen chapters may be read. The reading may also be collective, in which case the entire book is read by all or most of the people assembled. The other aspects of the *Poojā* remain the same as in Rāmāyana *Pāth.*

Navarātra : This particular *poojā* is largely an individual or family affair but in some parts of the country it is celebrated as a festival. *Navarātra* literally means a period covering nine nights. The adults in the family keep a semi-fast for nine days eating only fruits and vegetables. On the ninth day the fast is broken with formal worship of *Devi.* There are two *navarātras*, one in autumn, the other in spring. A festival marks the end of each. The autumn *navarātra* ends in the festival called *Dashaharā* or *Durgā Poojā*; the spring one ends in the celebration of *Rāmnavami* - the birthday of Rāma.

We have given a somewhat brief description of these *poojā*s in order to acquaint the reader with the rituals and the symbolism behind them. Many Hindu families outside India observe and celebrate these occasions and in order to carry on the tradition it is essential for the next generation to understand the place and significance of these performances in their cultural background.

CHAPTER TWO

FESTIVALS

Every society in every age has found ways to express their joys, sorrows, or gratitude by celebrating festivals. Most of the time the festivals are marked by exuberance even if the occasion is somber. Festivals bear the mark of a culture that evolves from the religion. They portray the arts, beliefs, and all other products of thought and action of a particular group. Festivals become a tradition in the society and are associated with particular days of the calendar. For example, Christmas is the most popular in Christianity. On the other hand, Thanksgiving celebrated in North America is probably the best example of festivity to express gratitude to God. Hinduism has a rich tradition of festivals. Some are celebrated on lavish scales, others may be more individualistic or family oriented. All the festivals fall on fixed days of the Hindu calendar in which the year begins in spring. All months have thirty days starting from the first day of the dark phase of the moon and ending at full moon. Every few years a year has thirteen months when one of the months is repeated.

Basant Panchami is the first festival of the year and celebrates the onset of spring. Saraswati, the goddess of learning is worshipped on this day and, therefore, students and educational institutions get involved in the celebration. It is customary to wear yellow dresses on this day. This festival is not associated with any event in mythology. The next major festival is *Holi*, the festival of colors. Families and friends visit each other and splash colors. People gather in streets and revel in the color bashing that goes on for most of the day. In villages there is a tradition of collective singing of *Holi* songs, which starts a couple of weeks before and ends on the day. The night before the revelry people burn a pile of wood collected over the past weeks in an open space. This is called *Holikā Dahan* and is associated with the story of a child devotee Prahlād. His father was as intensely anti-God as the son was devotee. His aunt Holikā had been granted the extraordinary power that fire could not burn her. The father and the aunt conspired to kill the boy; she took him in her lap and the father started a fire around them. A miracle happened, Prahlād came out unscathed but Holikā was burnt to ashes. The burning of the woodpile is supposed to commemorate that event. The revelry was also made popular by the legend of Krishna and his sweetheart Rādhā playing *Holi* in Gokul and Barsānā, where Krishna spent his childhood. *Holi* is celebrated in most of India except the south. There are several minor festivals during summer and the rainy season. The autumn *Navarātra* comes after the end of the rainy season. The female form of God– *Shakti* is worshiped for nine nights. Even though this festival is popularly known as *Durgā Poojā*, it is essentially *Devi Poojā*. *Shakti* has three forms, one stern and ferocious in the form of Durgā or Kāli, the other loving and generous in the form of Laxmi, and the last pure and serene in the form of Saraswati. The first three nights are devoted to the worship of Durgā for annihilating all the demonic and evil tendencies in us, the next three nights to Laxmi for prosperity, and the last three to Saraswati for knowledge and enlightenment. A large image or statue of Durgā is installed for the worship. The festival culminates in a daylong celebration and at the end the image is immersed in a river. This festival is most popular in the eastern parts of India.

The next major festival is Dashaharā which usually falls in the month of October. It is associated with the story of Rāmāyana. Dramas based on the life of Rāma are enacted in open-air theaters for ten days. The last day marks the end of the fight between *Rāma* and Rāvana. A huge effigy of Rāvana is erected and burnt at the end. In large towns there are special open fields earmarked for the event. The *Rāmlilā Maidān* in Delhi is an example. *Dashaharā* used to be the most lavishly celebrated festival in the pre-independence period because of the patronage of the rulers of the independent States. The event used to involve stately processions with caparisoned elephants and horses marching through the streets of the State capitals. The State of Mysore was famous for its *Dashaharā* celebrations.

Diwāli, the festival of lights follows almost at the heels of *Dashaharā*. It is also associated with the story of Rāma who returned home with Sitā and Laxman after fourteen years in exile and the city of Ayodhyā was lit up. *Diwāli* is also the day for worshiping Laxmi, the goddess of wealth. Sitā was the incarnation of Laxmi and the worship symbolically represents her coming into the homes of the devotees. Families decorate the inside and outside of their homes with lights. In cities prominent buildings are decorated lavishly in intricate patterns of light. This is also an occasion for firecrackers starting a few days earlier and ending late at night on Diwali day. In cities this raucous causes quite a few sleepless nights.

There are other festivals that are almost entirely religious in nature. *Rāmnavami* is the birthday of Rāma and is celebrated as a purely religious event. So is *Krishna Janmāshtami* celebrating the birth of Krishna. The Purāna devoted to the life of Krishna is *Bhāgavatam* and is called *Mahāpurāna,* i.e. the great *Purāna.* Krishna was born in jail, his parents having been jailed by his maternal uncle Kansa. He is the second incarnation of Vishnu in human form. He was born at midnight and it is customary to observe fast for the entire day and take food and drink only after midnight. Then there is *Shivarātri* associated with Shiva. There is a tradition of keeping an all night vigil in Shiva temples. It is believed that this is a recreation of an event in Shiva's life when he drank the deadly poison that came out from the ocean-churning in order to save the world. He was able to hold the poison in his throat and not let it go into his stomach. He became unconscious and his wife Pārvati spent the whole night holding his head until he gained consciousness. His throat became permanently blue and that is why he also goes by the name *Neelkantha.* There is another school of thought according to which *Shivarātri* celebrates the marriage anniversary of Shiva and Pārvati. Shiva Purāna does not shed any light on the origin of the festival but the first view seems more plausible. *Shivarātri* is also a day of fasting until the worship is over sometime during late evening or early night. These festivals are solemn occasions and are treated more like collective worships.

There is one festival that acquired a predominantly regional following in the late nineteenth century even though it had been an occasion of worship all over India. In religious context it is simply the worship of Ganesha but was relegated to a festival for social and political reasons. One of the prominent political leaders of the time B. G. Tilak saw the religious leanings of the people as a way to bring political awareness and inspired the people in the central parts of the country to take pride in their heritage. He popularized Ganesha Poojā in the form of *Ganapati* festival that provided a clarion call to the people of Mahārāshtra where it acquired the mark of identity and has since continued to be a regional tradition. Tilak was also a distinguished scholar of Hinduism. His treatise on Gitā, entitled *Gitā Rahasya* is one of the best.

There are other regional festivals that have little to do with religion and worship as such. *Pongal* is celebrated in Tamil region in January on *Makar Sankrānti* (after winter solstice). This is usually a three-day festival; the first day is devoted to domestic festivities, the second to honor the Sun god, and the third to the recognition of the role of cattle in man's life. *Onam* is a festival celebrated in Kerala and curiously it honors not a god but a demon king (*asur*) Bali. *Asuras* were professed enemies of *devas* (gods) even though both were children of Brahma. The Purānas are replete with the descriptions of battles between the two groups*.

According to the Purānic legend, this King Bali was learned, very pious, and famous for giving charities and for not denying any request for charity. This turned out to be his undoing as *Vāman* (the dwarf), who was the sixth incarnation of Vishnu, tricked him into giving all his possessions and kingdom in charity. He was then banished to a different land (Pātāl loka or nether region). The King was adored by his subjects and he also was very fond of

---

* Like everything else in Purānas the tales of *Devas* and *Asuras* are allegorical. The conflict between the two represents the constant struggle between the good and evil forces within a person or a society. On the surface the stories may seem ridiculous but the moral or the philosophy behind them is not.

them. When being exiled he asked Vishnu a favour — he should be allowed to visit his subjects once a year and his wish was granted. *Onam* marks the day of his yearly visit. It falls in autumn at the end of the southwest monsoon season. In the northern part of the country, there are also region-specific festivals like *Lohi* and *Vaisākhi* in Punjab.

The purpose of describing the main festivals here is to create the awareness that religion and culture are inseparable in any society, but in Hinduism they form the very fabric of life. It is also interesting to note that most of the festivals coincide with the harvesting seasons when people have natural tendencies to celebrate.

★ ★ ★

PART FOUR

PART FOUR

CHAPTER ONE

SYMBOLS

Symbols are an essential part of a religion. Every religion has at least one symbol that is distinctive and reveals its identity. As we have seen earlier, the rituals are also symbolic. With the immense diversity in the representation of God, symbolism is more prevalent in Hinduism. Even so the basic symbols represent the fundamental belief that God is one, formless, and infinite. These symbols are Om and Swastika. You find them displayed everywhere, in homes, temples, and on all special occasions.

Om is a synonym of God. The word was revealed to ancient sages in deep meditation as a sound reverberating within their bodies. Its chanting with proper pronunciation and stress produces the reverberations even in common people. That is why the chanting of Om is a sacred tradition. Its importance as a substitute name of God is demonstrated by the fact that an entire Upanishad* is devoted to the

---

*Māndukya Upanishad. It is the shortest and, perhaps, the most terse of the major *Upanishads*. The greatness of Om is described in other

exposition of this word. As a word Om has three parts — *A,U,M.* The sound of *A* is contained in every word that we speak and it is present everywhere. When *U* is pronounced after *A* the tendency is to raise the voice and the lips form a circular shape. In this posture *U* indicates the process of elevation. Finally in pronouncing *M* the lips come together at the end. The first part is symbolic of recognizing the omnipresent God within us, the second part represents the attempt to elevate the soul, and the third part completes the process of realization that only by elevating ourselves we can become one with God. There is another interpretation of these parts and both are philosophically related. There are three states of existence of a normal person. The first is the waking state, the second the dream, and the third deep sleep. Each part of Om is related to these states and the parts taken together represent the fourth state of existence when the soul in the body is in communion with the infinite of which the soul is a tiny part. Om is also represented as a symbol in the form of a separate alphabet. Here also it has three distinct parts. The main structure is the letter *A* but the left half of it is the letter *U.* The upper part in the form of a new moon and a dot above it, is the muted form of *M* * . In Sanskrit this symbol is a part of the alphabet. The three together form a distinct alphabet. Just as we use the names *A-kār* for sanskrit letter A and *U-kār* for U, the alphabet representing Om is called *Omkār.* Another synonym of *Om* is *Pranava.* The scriptures declare that *Om* is God and, therefore, the chanting of all mantras starts with *Om.* Of course the name can be, and is chanted by itself.

Upanishads also. *Shankarāchārya* also wrote a very short book on Om titled Panchikaranam.

*Sanskrit alphabet contains some symbols that represent part or truncated sounds of full alphabets. This particular symbol is called *'anunāsik'* or *'chandra bindu'.*

[OM]

अ + ऊ + म्

[A]   [U]   [M]

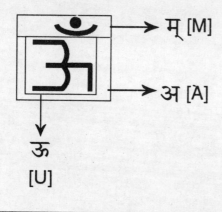

ॐ [OM-KAR]

म् [M]

अ [A]

ऊ
[U]

ॐ

[OM]

अ + उ + म

[M] [U] [A]

[OM-KAR] ॐ

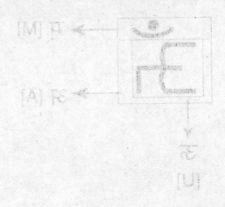

[M] म

[A] अ

[U] उ

As stated earlier the sound of Om was revealed, not created. This is a corollary of the basic belief of Vedanta philosophy that the universe is not a creation but manifestation of God. Om is universal. If we examine carefully the sounds used in other religions, we can see that all use this sound. Āmen in Christianity, Āmeen in Islam, Shalom in Judaism — all have the sound of Om.

Swastika is the oldest symbol in Hinduism. It probably originated with the concept of the Trinity and was meant to supplement the Shiva aspect of God. The word *swasti* (*su* meaning well + *asti* meaning be) means God bless you or be blessed, and is customarily used by people responding to the salutation by others. The suffix *ka* means the doer or giver; thus swastika means that which blesses and this leads us back to God. The symbol itself is supposed to bless the place and the people. There is ample evidence to show that it has been used in ages past by other cultures. Unfortunately the symbol has been defiled in the recent past and many people have come to associate it with exactly the opposite of what it is. It is not known* exactly what prompted Hitler to adopt it as a symbol of the Third Reich but people have to realize that a symbol does not lose its identity because it has been defiled. It is also pertinent to point out that there is a slight difference in the normal display of the symbol and its display as the Nazi emblem. In the Nazi version the symbol is rotated by an angle of

---

*Swastika was in use in Germany before Hitler. Towards the end of the nineteenth century some Volkists (racist cult) advocating the superiority of Aryan race or Herrenvolk (master race) adopted it as their symbol. By the beginning of the second decade of the twentieth century it had become the universal symbol of such groups. Dr. Friedrich Krohn, a dentist who belonged to one of these groups, designed the Nazi emblem for Hitler. A detailed discussion of Swastika's association with Hitler can be found in the book : 'Swastika and the Nazis' by Servando Gonzalez.

fortyfive degrees. Again we do not know if there was any significance to it.

There are different interpretations as to the structure of the symbol and why it represents blessing. Here we present the two — one philosophical, the other ritualistic. The symbol as a whole represents the wheel of time, the short segments perpendicular to the two axes at the ends denote the direction of the spin of the wheel. Time is unidirectional so all the short segments indicate a clockwise motion. A point on the wheel moves slower as it moves toward the center where the motion ceases. Thus the concept of time is relative, time stands still at the center, so the center is eternal. There is no beginning, there is no end. The universe begins as an expansion from the center and at the end collapses into it. This is the space-time singularity of modern astrophysics; the universe began with the big bang expansion and at some point it would start collapsing and end into the center. The center of the universe is the eternal truth — God, around whom everything revolves. The stronger our affinity to God, the faster we spiral towards the center and ultimately merge with Him. Those who are blessed go on that spiral. Material prosperity and happiness come from inner happiness. In a broader context Swastika is also God's emblem reiterating the fact that God is everywhere. The four horizontal and vertical lines represent the four cardinal directions; the perpendicular segments at the ends indicate the coverage of the non-cardinal directions. Swastika is usually painted in red, traditionally regarded as a sign of happiness and prosperity. Like the glow of the rising sun it sends forth the blessing to the people around.

The other explanation of the form of the symbol is related to the normal practice of worship of the planets (*navagraha pooja*). Apart from the various gods in Hinduism, there are

Swastika

Navagraha

⊙	⊙	⊙
KETU	MOON	MARS
⊙	⊙	⊙
RAHU	SUN	MERCURY
⊙	⊙	⊙
SATURN	VENUS	JUPITER

Swastika from Navagraha

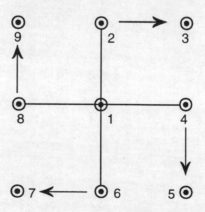

Swastika

Navagraha

MARS	MOON	KETU
MERCURY	SUN	RAHU
JUPITER	VENUS	SATURN

Swastika from Navagraha

nine astronomical entities that are also regarded as deities. These are the five planets visible to the naked eye (Mars, Mercury, Jupiter, Venus, Saturn), the sun, the moon, and the two ascending and descending nodes of the moon (Rāhu and Ketu pursuing the sun and the moon and causing eclipses; the nodes are the points on the moon's orbit when it lies in the same plane as the sun and the earth, the only times that eclipses can take place). In Hindu astronomy these nine are called *grahas* and regarded as planetary deities. In all traditional ceremonies these *grahas* are invoked and worshiped after Ganesha. They are represented by a three by three pattern of heaps of rice or beetle nuts with the sun placed at the center. The association between the nine *grahas* and Swastika becomes clear when we connect the nine points. Connecting the sun to the closest planets gives the two horizontal and vertical lines; then connecting the tips of these lines to the planet on the right side (clockwise direction) completes the symbol. The planets thus connected provide a more decorative pattern than the three by three configuration. The propitiation of the *grahas* is supposed to ward off evil influences and the symbol is therefore considered auspicious.

There are several other interpretations of the symbol in other parts of the world. A postcard version sees it as four L's joined at the apex signifying Luck, Light, Love and Life. Greek speaking people see it as four gammas. Others see the main frame as a cross and it is quite likely that the cross did evolve from it. There is ample evidence that Swastika has been used as a sign of good luck and blessing by different cultures in some form or other all over the world for several milleniums. It is ironic that its relatively short association with Hitler (about twelve years) has overshadowed its legitimate use from the very beginning of civilization.

★ ★ ★

With the multiplicity of gods and goddesses in Hinduism, images have a significant role in the lives of the devotees. Each image is distinct and even for a common man it is not difficult to recognize the particular god or goddess it represents. We need to remind ourselves again that the image is only a representation; we do not worship the image but the deity it represents and the deity in turn represents some aspect of God that we choose to worship. One might think that the original artist drawing the image had a free hand and used his imagination. But the images evolved from the description in the Purānas and just like the stories they also have two aspects, the visual and the philosophical. What we see may test our credibility but what lies behind the obvious is more important. It is not possible to discuss each and every deity and we will confine the discussion to the major figures. There are certain aspects of the images that are common. For example, the images of Shiva, Rāma, Krishna and Kāli are all depicted with their bodies in blue

Ten directions

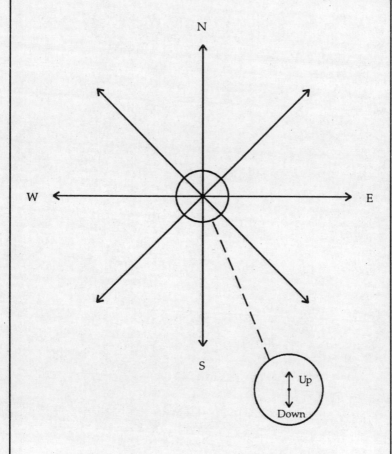

Multiple hands (4, 6, 8, 10) in images,
signify God's omnipresence.

Cardinal directions (4) + up and down (2) + corners (4) = 10

In Hindu astrology and rituals these ten directions
cover entire space.

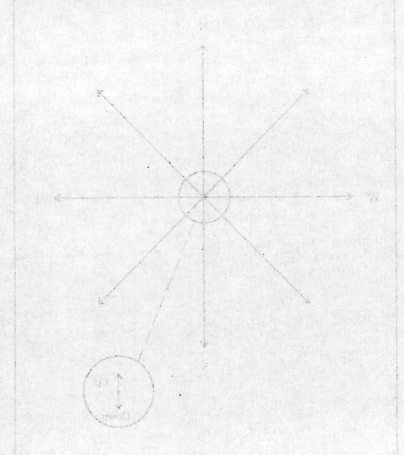

color. As stated repeatedly, the images represent God and hence strive to portray the fundamental concept of God. The sky is infinite, so is God. Everything we see is on the background of sky, the entire universe is a manifestation of the ultimate reality and the blue color is an assertion of that fact. Most of the images show four hands of the deity. In normal perception of the space around us we see it extending in all directions. God is omnipresent and is in every direction. The four hands signify the presence of God in all directions. In some images, especially of the goddesses, there are six, eight or ten hands. This is just an extension of the direction concept. If we add vertically up and down to the cardinal directions, we get six. We add the four directions midway between the cardinals, we get eight. We take all of the above, we get ten. A deity may have several names and sometimes even a slightly different image to go with the names.* Another distinctive feature of the representations is the mode of transportation for the deity, which is an animal or bird and is called *vāhan*. This is also symbolic and represents the vehicle through which the particular aspect of God is transferred to people. Each god or goddess has a unique *vāhan*.

Brahmā is the first of the Trinity and has the creator's role. As stated earlier, there are hardly any temples dedicated to him and he is not worshipped through images. However, he does have a pictorial representation. He is the only god shown with four heads. His four hands respectively hold *sruvā* (a straw-like thing to put *ghee* into the *Yajna* fire), Vedās (for imparting knowledge), *Kamandalu* (a water jug made from the shell of a special fruit for use at *yajna*), and a rosary signifying the unbroken bond between the soul and God. His *vahan* is swan (*hansa*) that has a legendary faculty of discrimination; it is supposed to be able to separate milk

---

* For example Durga, Shiva, Vishnu.

from water. Man can not have the power of creativity without having a strong sense of discrimination.

Vishnu is the next god in the Trinity, who has the task of maintaining the creation and of preserving the divine order. He is shown sitting on the back of *Sheshanāg*, the eternal serpent who, according to mythology, holds and supports the earth. The serpent also represents the universe that is in constant motion but outwardly tranquil, and God is overseeing it. In his four hands Vishnu holds a conch to spread the divine sound of *Om*, a discus to remind of the wheel of time and also to act as a weapon, a golden mace signifying the power to punish the wicked, and a lotus representing glorious existence. His *vāhan* is Garuda, the king of birds. In order to receive the blessings of Vishnu man has to be swift, fearless, and ready to give a helping hand to the needy; these are the qualities of Garuda. Vishnu goes by several other names, some of which are associated with specific temples. For example, in the famous Tirupati temple, he is enshrined as Venkateshwara where the image is also different. He is also worshiped as Satyanārāyana and again the image is slightly different. In fact *Vishnu* has one thousand names and it is customary to chant these names (*Vishnu sahasra nām*) at worships related to him in any form. Some other popular names are *Nārāyan* (one who lives on water), *Hari* (one who removes bondage), *Vishweshwar* (Lord of the universe) and so on. It is pertinent to note that Shiva also has a thousand names and most of the names are common for these two gods. This is not surprising considering the fact that they are not separate gods but different attributes of one God. This is also true for the three principal goddesses, as we shall see later. Vishnu is the only one of the Trinity to appear on the earth in various incarnations to save the world from destruction by evil

Brahmā

Brahma

TABLE OF APPENDICES · 77

Vishnu

Vishnu

Shiva

Natarāj

forces. There have been a total of ten incarnations; two in human form as Rāma and Krishna are famous.

Shiva completes the Trinity. He is associated with the dissolution of the universe but the word shiva means blessing and he has his benevolent side as well. He is usually shown sitting in meditation in a lotus position that is called *Siddhāsan* (posture of a realized person). He holds a trident, a drum (*damaru*), and a flaming torch in three hands; the fourth hand has palm thrust forward and outward signifying blessing.* The trident symbolizes the destruction of three types of miseries — physical, mental and spiritual. The drum symbolizes the sound of explosion at the destruction of the universe. The pose in meditation signifies the permanent calm that comes with realization of the self. There are more details in the image. Shiva has matted hair from which the river Ganges flows out. There is the crescent moon on the forehead and he has a third eye in between the two eyes; this eye is closed except when something or someone is to be destroyed. Finally he has a serpent coiled around his neck with its head erect and facing outward; the throat is blue. The matted hair represents the forest of ignorance in which knowledge can be easily lost. According to mythology when Bhagirath persuaded Ganges to come down to earth by his prolonged and intense penance, the earth was in danger of being swept away by the torrential flow. In order to save the earth Shiva held the Ganges in his hair and let it down in trickles. Ganges represents knowledge that has to be assimilated gradually. It can be easily lost in the forest of ignorance unless guided by divine will. The new moon symbolizes the beginning of this process that is gradual like its ascending phase. The snake symbolizes ego. An ego that is introvert can destroy the person; if it is extrovert it helps

---

* sometimes he is depected with only two hands especially when accompanied by Pārvati.

others. In the image the snake is always facing outward. Shiva also goes by several names; Shankar, Mahesh, Mahādeva are the popular ones. Some names are associated with famous temples like Vishwanāth in Vārānasi, Mahākāl in Ujjain, and Pashupati in Kāthmāndu. Shiva has another image as Natarāj. In this image he is shown in the role of destroyer performing the dance of destruction (*tāndava nritya*). Here he is shown in a dancing pose prancing on the body of a slain demon representing the destruction of all evil. We also have a unique representation of Shiva in *Shivalinga*. In almost all Shiva temples he is enshrined in this form. We discussed this aspect of *Shiva* worship earlier. Shiva's *vāhan* is a bull named Nāndi who represents hope, continuity, and strength. In the old days of agricultural society a bull belonged to the community as a whole and served the society, taking very little for its subsistence. It is this attitude of unselfish service that can bring lasting peace to mankind.

Saraswati is the consort of Brahma and hence the first member of the female Trinity worshipped as *Shakti*, the power of God. She is depicted as sitting on a lotus holding a book in one hand and playing *Veenā* (an instrument akin to violin) with two hands. The fourth hand is extended palm outwards in a gesture of blessing. She is dressed in white which denotes purity. The lotus seat signifies glorious existence, the book symbolizes knowledge, and the *veenā* indicates outflow of music and love. She is the goddess of learning, intellect, and art. Her *vāhan* is the swan, the same as *Brahma's*. *Laxmi* is the consort of Vishnu and is the goddess of wealth and prosperity. She sits on a lotus and holds a lotus flower and a conch in her upper hands; the right lower hand is extended outwards with the palm facing the devotees and gold coins keep pouring from her fourth

Saraswati

Saraswati

Laxmi

Pārvati meditating

hand. These attributes signify purity, chastity, generosity, and accessibility. Her *vāhan* is also *Garuda*, the same as *Vishnu's*. Vishnu has had two incarnations in human form, in which *Laxmi* also incarnated to keep him company. The third member of the female Trinity is Pārvati. She is Shiva's wife and is the only one whose marriage is described in mythology. She has different representations depending on which of her images is being looked at. She is fierce and powerful in the form of Durgā or Kāli. Here she is presented as the destroyer of the demons and evil. She has eight hands all carrying some weapon. She rides a lion that is her *vāhan*. The lion symbolizes absence of fear, courage, and strength. These are the qualities through which man can destroy the evils within and around him. As Kāli her body is portrayed in black color, her tongue thrust out and dripping blood, and carrying the severed head of a demon in one hand. The word Durgā means hard to reach *(dukhen gantum shakya iti Durga)* Kāli means black. This form of Devi is worshiped for the destruction of all the evil tendencies within us. As is the case with most *Purānic* descriptions, the terms demon and evil are allegorical. For man to approach God the evil in him has to be destroyed. As the wife of Shiva she is depicted as a gracious worldly woman sitting beside her husband. The name Pārvati comes from mythology; she is supposed to be the daughter of the great mountain Himālaya (Parvat's daughter). In an earlier incarnation she was the daughter of *Prajāpati* Daksha and her name was *Sati.* She got married to Shiva. In one of his famous *Yajna, Daksha* insulted Shiva, Sati could not take it, and burnt herself producing fire by sheer will power. In revenge Shiva destroyed the kingdom of Daksha and became ascetic. In her incarnation as Pārvati she started doing intense penance for getting her husband back but he was in no mood to become a householder again. Her mother asked her to desist from treating her body so severely. One day in the presence of her playmates she asked her not to (*Umā* in Sanskrit, U- form of address, mā - don't). Her friends thought that the mother was calling her by her name. Since then her alternate name became Uma.* Since Shiva was not paying much attention to Pārvati, the gods got into the act and asked Kāmdeva (cupid) to try his famous arrow. While he was trying to aim the arrow, Shiva opened his third eye and Kāmdeva got burnt to ashes. After this episode Pārvati did manage to get Shiva's attention and they finally got married. Pārvati is worshiped by married women for long happy married life. Another name by which Pārvati was known before marriage is Gauri which is also associated with mountain (*giri*). Unmarried girls worship Gauri for obtaining desirable husbands. At the beginning of marriage ceremonies *Gauri* is worshiped along with Ganesha.

We have already talked about the origin of Ganesha and the symbolism associated with the story. In the images he is sitting leisurely on the ground with his large stomach protruding. In his hands he carries an axe and a rope (to cut and remove all obstacles), a sweet ball made of flower (*modak* to reward the devotees), while the fourth hand is open and thrust forward in the act of blessing. The trunk dropping between the two tusks is bent inward and one of the tusks is broken. The names *Vakratunda* and *Ekadanta* derive from these features, while the name *Lambodar* comes from his huge stomach. The two tusks represent the opposite natures, good and evil and the trunk passing between the two represents the power of discrimination. The tusk representing evil is broken signifying that with the blessing of God good always prevails over evil. The large

---

* This anecdote is in Kumārsambhavam, one of the celebrated works of Kālidās(U.26)

Ganesha

stomach symbolizes the capacity to devour and digest all knowledge. The name *Vināyak* comes from this attribute. Lying in front of him on the carpet is an open book signifying his constant endeavor to assimilate and impart knowledge. There is also a plate full of sweets and a little mouse sitting beside the plate with its tail quivering and looking longingly at the sweets but not daring to touch them. The mouse is Ganesha's *vāhan* — seemingly a most undesirable combination considering the bulky figure of Ganesha. The mouse can put away a large amount of food, several times its own weight, in a hurry. It is known to deplete entire bushels of grain overnight. The mouse also represents desire. An uncontrolled desire for material prosperity can lead a man to disaster. On the other hand, man can achieve great things with controlled desire. The mouse with quivering tail symbolizes controlled desire. He dare not touch the sweets without the lord's permission. Ganesha is the god of riches and achievements (*riddhi siddhi*) that can be bestowed only upon men with controlled desire and absence of greed.

From *Purānās* we come to the Epics. *Rāmāyana*, as discussed before, is the story of *Rāma* originally written by sage Vālmiki. Rāma is the incarnation of Vishnu and his wife Sitā is the incarnation of Laxmi. The other characters in the story are also incarnations of various gods and goddesses. Temples have been especially built and dedicated to Rāma even though he is essentially the human form of Vishnu. But just for that reason his image is different. He is a man with two hands and no special symbols are attached to his image. Usually Sitā is beside him. He was an ideal man from beginning to end - a devoted son, affectionate brother, ideal husband, and a true friend. He was also an ideal ruler; his reign (*Rāma Rājya*) is synonymous with ideally happy and prosperous conditions. Yet he was human and *Valmiki* has allowed him some human frailties. He was instrumental in killing Bāli treacherously. At the end of the war with Rāvana, Sitā is brought back to him but he does not want to accept her purity unless she goes through the fire test. At this strange behavior of his the gods, including Brahmā, appear and exhort him as Vishnu and tell him that the action does not behoove him. He replies : "I consider myself a man, son of Dasharath; if you think I am someone else, tell me." Sitā goes through the fire test and comes out unscathed. Yet back in his kingdom, when he finds that she is pregnant, he deserts her just because of some lowly gossip. In his version of the story Tulsidās never forgets the fact that Rāma is God incarnated and incapable of doing anything wrong. That the masses also take that view, is shown by the popularity of the Rāma temples. There are several holy places associated with Rāma's travel and these are treated as pilgrimages.

Krishna is the other incarnation of Vishnu. Bhāgavatam - the *Mahāpurāna* is devoted to his life. For the masses though he is more often remembered through Mahābhārata and Bhagavad Gitā embedded in it. The images of *Krishna* are many: as a child, as a cowherd boy in Gokul with his inseparable flute, dancing with *Gopi's* in Brindāvan, frolicking with and teasing his sweetheart Rādhā, as the chariot driver of Arjuna preaching him Gitā, and so on. The images in the temples mostly depict him holding the flute to his lips and standing on one leg with the other leg bent upward and touching it. The symbolism of the flute is that God breathes life into every living creature; one foot firmly planted on the ground and the other indicating motion symbolize the fact that God is immovable, unaffected by time while the universe is in motion and subject to changes.

Rāma

Rāma

Krishna

Krishna

Durgā

Kāli

KALI.

Unlike Rāma, Krishna declares himself to be the embodiment of God on several occasions. All the same, his life was more down to earth because he grew up as a commoner and was more accessible to people around him. There was no aura associated with him even in his later life. He was born in unusual circumstances involving miracles attributed to his divine status; in fact his whole life is replete with supernatural events. One of the unusual events in his life is the so-called *Rāslilā*. where he dances with a large number of *Gopis* (milkmaids) under moonlight and each *Gopi* thinks that he is dancing with her alone. This event is enacted every year during the autumn *Navarātra* festival especially in Gujrāt and Rājasthān. The philosophical meaning behind *Rāslilā* is the relationship between the individual soul and God, the infinite source of the souls (the word for soul is ātmā and one of the names of God is *Paramātmā*, i.e. the supersoul). *Gopis* symbolize the individual souls and the dance represents the interplay between the soul and God in its quest to merge with Him. The most famous Krishna temples are in Mathura, Gokul, and Brindāvan where he spent his childhood, and in Dwārakā, the capital of his kingdom. Krishna goes by several names. Some of the popular ones are Gopāl (protector of cows), Murlidhar (holder of flute), Ghanshyām (having the dark color of clouds), Vāsudeva (son of Vasudeva), Yogeshwar (lord of yoga) and so on.

In the hierarchy of gods Hanumān, the so-called monkey god, has a unique place. He is included in the list because he is worshiped as a god and there are temples dedicated to him all over India. He is an important character in Rāmāyaṇa and was the most ardent devotee of Rāma, always ready to serve him. He is idolized as a stepping stone for reaching God in the form of Rāma. This came about largely because towards the end of Rāmāyana Rāma says that his devotees are dear to him but the devotees of the devotees are dearer. Since Hanumān is his first and foremost devotee, he becomes a direct link to God. Besides devotion, Hanumān represents courage, hope, and intellect. He remained celibate throughout his life and for that reason he is revered by students who are in the first *(brahmacharya)* stage of life. Because of his physical strength he is the favorite god of wrestlers. The images in the temples show him ready to spring holding a mace in his hand. Sometimes he is also shown with Rāma enshrined in his heart. Another popular picture shows him flying through air holding up the mountain that contained the life saving herb for Laxman. This depicts an episode from Rāmāyana when in the war with Rāvana, Laxman is wounded. According to mythology Hanumān is son of *Vāyu*, the air god (another word for air is *Pavan* and Hanumān is also known as *Pawansut* (son of *Pavan*). He is supposed to drive away all the difficulties of the devotees; this is reflected in the name *Sankatmochan*. Another popular name for him is Mahāvir. Hanumān also appears in Mahābhārata but by that time he is quite old. Bhima, one of the *Pāndavas* was also son of *Vāyu* and, therefore, Hanumān's younger brother. There is an anecdote where Bhima meets Hanumān and finally recognizes him as his elder brother when the Pāndavas are roaming in forests in exile. He is also shown sitting on the top of Arjuna's chariot driven by Krishna during the war.

CHAPTER THREE

SAMPRADĀYA'S
(Denominations within Hinduism)

As a religion and the associated culture develop, religious leaders with slightly different ideas or interpretation of facts tend to gather their followers thus forming different groups within the same religion. Since Hinduism is based on philosophy, the differences in regard to details are many. The root scriptures are *Vedās* and the writings therein are subject to varied interpretations especially because of aphorism that is extensively used. Just after the Vedic period there were six different schools of philosophy all claiming the Vedās as the source. Vedānta was the one that finally emerged as the foundation of *Sanātan Dharma*, the actual name of the religion. Subsequently, differences in interpretation arose even within Vedānta. Masters propounding their own understanding of the scriptures developed their own following but the grouping was purely at the intellectual level. Meanwhile there were reformist movements which considered the difference between the theory and practice of the religion objectionable. They developed their own followings and became separate groups. In the Purānic age, for example, the devotees of Vishnu and Shiva formed different groups. They were called *Vaishnava* and *Shaiva* respectively. This was the emergence of the so-called *sampradāyas* in Hinduism. For the lack of an exact word to convey the meaning in English we will call them denominations. Later on several other denominations came into existence because of dissatisfaction with the status quo or for asserting the uniqueness of particular groups. The best known among these are Jainism and Buddhism that are even regarded as separate religions. This was the beginning of a new trend where the person became more important than the fundamental beliefs. For example, Gautam rebelled against the existing practices of the religion and went on his own in the search of eternal truth. Through his individual effort he became Buddha. He did not believe in God in the same way as others. Yet his followers made him God. This is of course an extreme example but on smaller scales the trend continued. The followers of some of these groups believe and, sometimes openly declare, that their preceptors were incarnations of gods.

The word *sampradāya* has been used in different senses. For example, even up to present there is a *Nāgā sampradāya* whose members believe in walking naked or almost naked. They can be seen having their own procession in large religious festivals and fairs. They do not have any leader whom they adore and worship. Swami Dayānanda started Ārya Samāj but his followers never attributed divinity to him. On the other hand, Chaitanya attracted a considerable following and at least some of his followers consider him an incarnation. Even Rāmakrishna is considered an incarnation by some of his followers. Here we want to discuss the groups that follow their leader almost with blind faith (and we do not mean to use the adjective 'blind' in a derogatory sense.) All these groups are in the mainstream of Hinduism and have, in their own way, done much good for the community in general. Yet, in some, there is an element of rigidity involved in their thinking, which leads to a sense of intolerance for differing views. All believe in the same basic principles, only the interpretations are different and the ways of implementation in daily life are divergent. Each of these groups started as followers of some religious person in India and, except for one, all started there. With the migration of Hindus to the west these groups started functioning outside India as well. The groups can be broadly classified as philosophic, ritualistic, and related to yoga.

J. Krishnamurti, who did not believe in any organized path for reaching God, preached the most abstract form of Vedānta philosophy. In fact he did not believe in God in the normal accepted sense. For him God was the eternal truth which is ''a pathless land and you can not approach it by any path whatsoever.'' One can realize the truth only by making his mind free from conditioning of race, nationality, religion, dogma, tradition, opinion etc., which inevitably lead to conflict. Thus he did not believe in religion even though philosophically his ideas were Vedāntic. He was born in 1895 and the Theosophical Society leader Annie Bessant influenced his childhood and student days. Later he broke away from every tradition and preached his philosophy of eternal truth and the need for free mind. He came to be recognized as one of the great thinkers of the twentieth century and developed a large following in 'intellectual circles'. He spent most of his life in Europe and died in 1986. Even though he was against forming organizations, Krishnamurti Foundations sprang up all over the world to carry on his legacy. He wrote several books expounding his views and his lectures have been compiled in the form of books.

The next organization in this group is *Rāmakrishna Mission* which was founded by Swāmi Vivekānanda towards the end of the nineteenth century to propagate the teachings of his Guru Rāmakrishna Paramhansa. Rāmakrishna himself was illiterate. Born as Gadādhar Chatopādhyāya in a poor Brāhmin family in West Bengal, he had no liking for school. Not able to find any other work he joined his elder brother who was the priest at Kāli temple at Dakshineshwar near Calcutta. When his brother died a few years later he became the priest in charge of the temple. As if to make up for the lack of knowledge he became extremely religious in his outlook and became an ardent devotee of Mother Kāli. He also learnt *tāntric* practices from a woman ascetic called Bhairavi Brāhmini and took to austerities that included fasting, meditation, and constant chanting of mantrās. Later he learnt Vedānta from a *Sādhu* named Totāpuri. Thus, even though he himself could not read the scriptures, he became its teacher and expounded his ideas to select gatherings. It was towards the end of his life that, in a trance, he told his disciples : "What was Rāma, what was Krishna, that is what I am" and that is how he got the name Rāmakrishna. He became famous more through his disciple Narendranāth Dutta, who later came to be known as Vivekānanda and started the Mission named after his guru. The emphasis of this group is on Vedānta, although there is a certain amount of ritualistic flavor as the members almost worship Rāmkrishna. The mission has several centers in the West, especially in America. It has an established order of monks and *Brahmchāris* (understudies aspiring to be monks) who carry out the mission work. Their followers come from all segments of the society, as the mission believes that Hinduism is a way of life; any one can become a Hindu and no formal conversion is required. The Mission has its own publication division that publishes original scriptures as well as books dealing with the life and teachings of Rāmakrishṇa and Vivekānanda.

Another organization that works towards the spiritual uplift of mankind is Chinmaya Mission. Their goal is to provide individuals from any background the wisdom of *Vedānta*. Swami Chinmayānanda was one of the most famous religious personalities of the twentieth century. He was from Kerala but had his university education in the north. After finishing his education he became disenchanted with the worldly life and decided to become a *sanyāsi* (monk). He developed a large following as he preached the essence of Hinduism. He started a formal base at Mumbai called Sandipan Ashram named after the legendary *guru* of Krishna and Sudāma. His sphere of influence extended to the West in the sixties and seventies. He also started a much-needed program to teach the children of first generation Hindu immigrants the basics of Hinduism. The schools called *Vāl Vihār* are a part of Chinmaya centers whose number has multiplied since his death in 1993.

A different group that comes under the Vedānta umbrella and deserves mention here is that of Arbindo followers. Arbindo Ghosh was born in 1872 in a well-to-do family of Calcutta; his father was a surgeon who had obtained his MD degree in Scotland. He sent his son for schooling to England at a very young age hoping that the son would get into the Indian Civil Service. Even though Arbindo was a brilliant student, he did not get into the Civil Service because he could not pass the horse-riding course. Instead he turned into a radical revolutionary and after returning to India became involved in the movement to throw the British out of the country. He was arrested a couple of times and spent almost a year in jail in 1908. While in prison he studied Bhagavad Gitā and Upanishads and 'found himself' through the spiritual guidance from the scriptures. Soon after he openly declared having washed his hands off politics but that apparently did not convince the authorities. In order to avoid another arrest he fled into nearby Chandernagar, a French possession, and from there to another French enclave, Pondicheri, way down south. He had a sudden desire to put his newly found spirituality into practice and started a place for spiritual activities giving daily discourses. This became the Arbindo Āshram. His teachings were philosophical with special emphasis on yoga and meditation; in fact he later came to be called *Mahāyogi* (great yogi). He attracted followers from all over. One of his devotees was a Mrs. Richard whom he had known in England. She moved to the Āshram and became his confidant and assistant. She came to be called the Mother. Arbindo Āshram also publishes books expounding his views on Hinduism and Vedānta philosophy. During the last years of his life he went into seclusion and was accessible to no one but the Mother except for his occasional but brief public appearances to give *darshan* to the devotees. The Mother became the head of the organization after his death in 1950. She came to be venerated almost as much as the master. She died in 1973 but the activities at the Āshram continue with followers all over the world.

Among the ritualistic groups the most prominent and visible are Hare Krishnas. They are often seen at airports and other public places selling books and flowers and are conspicuous with clean-shaved heads (men only) and traditional Indian dresses. This is the only group that first flourished outside India although it had been started in India by Swami Prabhupad whose preceptor lineage goes back to Chaitanya in the seventeenth century. He started the International Society of Krishna Consciousness (ISKCON) and initially his followers were almost all non-Indians. Since their spiritual tie was with India, the places associated with Krishna's life became favorite pilgrimages and centers were started there and later in other parts of the country. *Krishna* is their supreme deity and their temples are dedicated to Rādhā and Krishna (as well as to his wife Rukmini). They follow the traditional Hindu ways of life, strict daily routines and are all dedicated to the service of Krishna. The large centers have an agricultural base as well and maintain farms for milk and food production. They also have schools for children based on the ancient system of *Gurukul*; the children are away from the parents and follow strict discipline. Hare Krishnas consider Prabhupad as the last incarnation of Vishnu and venerate him as such. The movement spread rapidly in America and Europe and they have centers all over the world. Prabhupad wrote treatises on the scriptures and other books. Bhagavad Gitā and Bhāgavatam are, of course, his books of choice. His explanations, though, are always subjective and sometimes stretched too far to accommodate the beliefs of the group. The society maintains its own publication division and the books are informative if you ignore the stretched purports. It must be said however, that they contributed significantly in making Hinduism better known and accepted in the western world.

The other group in this class is Saibābā's. The followers of Saibābā are ritualistic in the sense that they worship him and believe in his capability to perform miracles. The original Saibābā was a simple hermit who lived around

Aurangābād in Central India. Impressed by his miracles one of his devotees took him to a small place called Shirdi and he stayed there. He believed that God performed the miracles through him; he gave comfort to his devotees through healing and moral guidance. One of his rich devotees was building a temple for Krishna; Saibābā helped in designing it but died before its completion. The devotee dedicated the temple to him and he was buried there. (In some parts of India sanyāsis and hermits are not cremated, they are placed underground in the eternal state of bliss (*chirsamādhi*). In his case, however, no one knew for certain whether he was Hindu or Muslim). Every year thousands of devotees go to the shrine and special festivals are held there. The story of Saibābā does not end there though. Another Saibābā appeared in Banglore who claims to be the incarnation of the original one. He is also said to perform miracles and has a large following in India as well as abroad. There have been controversies surrounding him but devotees believe in him and his following has increased steadily.

There is another group that is rather regional in character in the sense that it started in Gujarāt and the following is largely within that region. Its extension into the West is also along the same lines. It started with a small number of admirers of Swaminarāyana who preached the basic tenets of Hinduism from the point of view of the path of devotion. His popularity grew and he became somewhat of a legend. The group formulated its own code of behavior and after his death Swaminarāyana temples sprang up. With the migration to other parts of the world his devotees have established centers and temples in different places. As it happens in most cases of personality exaltation, the emphasis shifted from the basics of the religion to the person himself.

The denominations in the third category are related to yoga. Even though in the West yoga is generally associated with physical exercises, it is a philosophy — one of the six principal schools of philosophy mentioned earlier. It was annunciated by Pātanjali and his *Yogasutra* is the source book. The physical part called hathayoga is only a way of conditioning the body for developing a healthy mind. Meditation is an essential part of yoga and also the ultimate means of self-realization. It has been practiced for spiritual as well as physical well-being. Although yoga had been introduced to the western world at the turn of the century, it became popular only in the late sixties and seventies. Some accomplished practitioners of yoga came out of India and established yoga schools and institutes and got good recognition. Books on the subject became freely available and even the word yoga was assimilated in the English language. One of the movements organized during the early stages of this resurgence of yoga was *Ānanda Mārg*, the path of bliss. It was founded in 1955 in a small town in Bihār by a commoner rather than any well-known religious personality. Its aim was the spiritual and social uplift of mankind in general. Yoga and meditation were the starting point in the process of spiritual advancement but the path of knowledge was also stressed. Like Rāmakrishna Mission it also developed its own order of monks and soon the organization extended into other parts of the world. Although the basic tenets are of Hinduism, the organization claims to follow no particular religion, rather a universal religion that may be called human religion (*mānava dharma*). They do have the missionary spirit and the centers organize regular yoga classes and hold retreats and special gatherings to bring together the devotees. There is a large emphasis on collective meditation. The order allows women also to be monks and every center has followers who work full time for the mission or are apprentices for becoming monks if they choose so. They also have their own publications propounding their views on Vedanta philosophy and the scriptures. The founder, P. R. Sarkār has written a number of books. The organization also runs a number of social welfare programs in India as well as outside.

One of the earliest yoga missionaries was Swami Yogānanda who came to America in the early twenties. He belonged to an order of yogis claiming their lineage to one legendary guru (Baba Ji) who lived centuries ago. This order believes in what is known as Kriyā Yoga. The word *kriyā* means an action in progress. This branch of yoga focuses on life force and breath control (*prānayām*) and also emphasizes the role of sound and music in spirituality. The goal is to achieve perfection through practice culminating in a pulseless, breathless state of meditation called *nirvikalpa samādhi* (a state that remains constant). Yogānanda's autobiography (Autobiography of a Yogi) became very popular and is still considered one of the best expositions of yoga philosophy. It has been published in seventeen languages. There are several Kriyā Yoga centers especially in Europe and America. Strictly speaking this is not a separate denomination but it does have a unique place among the groups actively seeking spiritual advancement.

Finally there is the ancient sect of *tāntriks*. *Tantra* is essentially a separate branch of yoga that developed in the Purāṇic age and involves various occult practices in the pursuit of spiritual advancement. It has a separate set of sacred books and Shiva and Shakti are the principal deities. *Āgama* is one of the source books and it deals with rites, dharma, and cosmology. There are various subsects within the group and some are ascetics following bizarre practices. Some put equal emphasis on yoga and *bhoga* (enjoyment).

There are several *Tantra yoga* centers scattered throughout the world but most of them are not involved in occult practices. The kings of Chandela dynasty, who built the temple complex in Khajuraho during the period 950 to 1050 AD, were supposed to be followers of tantra tradition. There are different views about the carvings on those temples and there may be a deeper meaning to the erotic scenes depicted there.

This discussion of *sampradāyas* is not intended to be all-inclusive. There are several other groups, both within India and outside, working towards spiritual and social uplift of Hindus in general. Some of these are not sectarian at all. They work through volunteers in geographically limited areas. A recent group is the Svādhyāya group started by Pāndurang Shāstri in Mahārāshtra and Gujarāt. This is not to be confused with Svādhyāya Mandal started by Sātawalekar in Pāradi, Gujarāt, which is more of an academic center.

PART FIVE

PART FIVE

CHAPTER ONE

A BRIEF INTRODUCTION TO SCRIPTURES

Hinduism has its origin in the *Vedās* that propound its basic philosophy and beliefs. *Vedās* are not books in the conventional sense, since they are compilations of the accumulated experiences of a large number of sages over several centuries. There are four of them - Rigveda, Yajurveda, Sāmaveda and Atharvaveda. However, *Yajurveda* has two separate branches - Krishna Yajurveda and Shukla Yajurveda. Each Veda consists of four parts; *Samhitās, Brāhmans, Āranyaks* and Upanishads. At present, however, when we look for the books, the title Veda refers only to the *Samhitās*. For example, the book Rigveda is just Rigveda Samhitā. The Samhitās contain the mantrās and are mostly in the form of relatively short poems called *richās*. The Brāhmans are explanations of the ideas contained in the *richās* and are mostly in prose. The Āranyaks are discussions of the mantrās and their significance in the form of dialogs and discussions. Upanishads are collections of the main philosophical parts of the Vedās and are not separate entities.

Since Vedanta philosophy is based on the Upanishads, these are also referred to as Vedanta. That confuses some people in believing that Upanishads are the last parts of the Vedās because the word vedānta literally means the end of Vedās. The syllable *ved* means knowledge and *anta* means end; the combined word means the end or culmination of knowledge. The Upanishads have been taken from the Brāhmans and Āranyaks, the only exception being Ishopanishad which is from Shukla Yajurveda Samhitā. There are twelve major Upanishads and several minor ones; the total number is supposed to be one hundred and eight but the authenticity of some of them is doubtful. Since the vedās (and hence the Upanishads) were compiled by different sages over several centuries, there are overlapping and apparently contradictory statements in them. In order to clarify these statements another book was written by a sage named Bādarāyana. It is generally believed that the prolific author and sage *Vyās* wrote it under this pseudonym. The book is *Brahmasutra* but it also goes by the name *Vedāntasutra*. It is a collection of aphorisms referring to specific portions of the Upanishads.

As stated in one of the Upanishads (Mundak, 1.1. 4-5), there are two kinds of knowledge, one higher (*parā*) and the other lower (*aparā*). The higher one is the knowledge of Brāhman (God), by knowing which everything else is known; the lower one consists of the material contained in the vedās — phonetics, ritual, grammar, etymology, metrics, and astronomy — the so-called six *vedāngas* or limbs of vedās. Both are fully contained in the vedās, one implicitly the other explicitly. Originally these subjects had to be learned in vedic schools in order to understand the vedic texts. Subsequently these subjects were treated more systematically in separate special schools devoted to the six supplementary sciences of vedās. This led to the development of special texts in the form of *sutras* to help memorization. The literal meaning of *sutra* is thread and denotes a succinct rule condensed into a few words. A system of instructions is compiled from the *sutras* and the collection itself is called *sutra*, since it threads through the entire subject. The *sutras* were a pragmatic solution to the problem of dissemination of knowledge in the absence of printed material. In the words of Winternitz "there is probably nothing like these *sutras* in the entire literature of the world. It is the task of the author of such a work to say as much as possible in as few words as possible, even at the expense of clearness and intelligibility." The origin of the *sutra* literature can be traced to the Brāhman part of the vedās. Since this part dealt mostly with ritual, it was the first vedānga to which *sutras* were devoted. This literature is known as Kalpasutra (*kalpa* means ritual). Kalpasutrās dealing with the general rituals taught in *Brāhmans* are called *Shrautsutras*, while those dealing with the domestic ceremonies are called *Grihyasutrās* and the rituals for all religious ceremonies and *samskārs* are contained in these sutras. Other vedāngas also had separate *sutrās* devoted to them. The best known of these are Pāninisutra for grammar and Pātanjali Yogasutra for yoga. Shulvasutra, which is essentially a part of Shrautsutras, describes the rules for measurements of fire altars (*yajna kund*) and for building the place for the yajnas (*yajna shala*). These are perhaps the oldest work of geometry and architecture.

Immediately after the Vedic period six different schools of philosophy developed, each taking Vedās as the starting point. These were - *Purva Mimānsā*, *Nyāya*, *Vaisheshik*, *Sāmkhya*, Yoga and Uttar *Mimānsā*. Later on the last one came to be known as Vedānta. Each was started by a venerated sage and had considerable following. Even now they are a part of the ancient Hindu literature and are collectively referred to as *Khatdarshan* (six philosophies). With time Vedānta became the most popular one and incorporated some of the main aspects of *Sāmkhya* and Yoga. One of the main contributors to this integration was Vyās who tried to summarize the teachings of the Upanishads in Mahābhārata in the form of a dialog between Krishna and Arjun at the start of the war. This part of the Epic consisting of eighteen chapters was later given an independent status as Bhagavad Gitā (although it is still a part of Mahābhārata) and came to be regarded on par with Upanishads. Thus the Upanishads, Brahmasutra and Bhagavad Gitā together became the foundation of *Vedānta* and are known as *Prasthān Trayi* (three starting points or three foundation stones).

Up to this point the concept of God was purely abstract. As discussed earlier, in order to bring religion within the grasp of the common man the principal deities came into being and another branch of literature grew with the proliferation of gods and goddesses. These books were known as Purānas. It must be emphasized, however, that even in the Purānas the one all-pervading, all-powerful God remained as the backdrop of the deity they were extolling. This is evident from the prayers contained in all of them. They dealt with specific deities and tried to convey the teachings of the Vedās through stories. There are one hundred and eighteen Purānas. One dealing with the life of Shri Krishna is Shrimad Bhāgavatam and is known as Mahāpurāna, i.e. the supreme Purāna. The two main epics Rāmāyana written by Vālmiki and Mahābhārata written by Vyās also appeared during this period. Both attempted to summarize the teachings of the Vedās and principal Purānas through sub-stories in the general context of the main story. Rāmāyana is basically the life story of Rāma who was the first incarnation of Vishnu in human form. Mahābhārata is the story of conflict and war between two groups of cousins — Pāndavās and Kauravās, and includes a substantial part of the life of Krishna, the second human incarnation of Vishnu. Allegorically it describes the conflict between the forces of good and evil constantly going on within the human body. Mahābhārata is a gigantic literary masterpiece and covers almost every facet of human life. It is so all-embracing that, after writing the epic, Vyās made a sweeping statement that 'whatever is here may be found elsewhere, but what is not here can not be found anywhere else'.* The story of Rāmāyana was subsequently written in several regional languages. Although the story remained essentially the same in all these versions, these books were not translations of Vālmiki Rāmāyana. One written in Hindi by Tulsidās became very popular and is often called Rāmāyana although the actual name of the book is Rāmacharit Mānas. Mahābhārata has not been rewritten in the same sense but has been translated in several regional languages. For the bulk of the population the two epics form the bulwark of Hinduism.

There was another category of religious literature that appeared during and shortly after the Purānic period. These books laid down the code of conduct for Hindus and were called *Smritis*-although this word has also been used to indicate all religious literature other than Vedās. The most famous among these is Manusmriti written by Manu. Another set of books described in detail the procedures for rituals to be performed in daily life and on special occasions; these are known as Sutrās. The entire religious literature is

---

*Yadihāsti tadanyatra, yannehāsti na kutrachit.

collectively known as *Shāstrās*, a term that is widely used. Finally, we need to mention two books that are not directly related to religion but deal with human nature. The first one is Hitopadesh, the literal meaning of which is teachings for general good. It deals with the human nature and ways to balance the strict codes of conduct enjoined by *Smritis* and the social and political needs of day to day life. The other book is Panchtantra. It deals with the same subjects as Hitopadesh but presents the teachings in the form of animal stories. The stories are popular with children but the philosophy is for everyone. The book has been translated in several western and even oriental languages.

All the scriptures were written in Sanskrit. As centuries passed, Sanskrit ceased to be the language of the people and several regional languages developed in different regions of India. Most of these are derived from Sanskrit but some are not. But everywhere in the country the language for conducting religious ceremonies and rites has continued to be Sanskrit through milleniums. For the priestly class the study of Sanskrit had been obligatory but the teaching of the language in schools had continued uninterrupted and a sizeable portion of the population can read it. In recent years there has been a concerted effort to revive it as a spoken language but it is too early to anticipate results.

The lofty ideas of Vedanta got sidetracked during and after the Purāṇic age and the religion started to become mostly ritualistic controlled by the priest class. Many negative elements like the degeneration of the caste system took hold of the society. It was at this stage that some sections of the populace rebelled against the development of religious hierarchy within Hinduism and reformist movements like Buddhism sprang up. Contrary to the popular belief,

Buddhism is not a separate religion but only an offshoot of Hinduism. The general public embraced Buddha's teachings because he tried to do away with the rigid class distinction and emphasized the simple and ascetic views of the Vedic period. He used the language of the common man (Pāli, also known as Prākrit) instead of the officially accepted language of the scriptures. In his lifetime at least the word *Dhammam* that he used in his famous initiation mantras* meant the prevailing Hindu *dharma*. In any case his following spread like wildfire mostly because of the general dissatisfaction of the people with the ritualistic practices. This was a wakeup call to the intelligentsia and a renaissance of the Vedanta philosophy began. The most prominent among those leading the charge against the spread of Buddhism was Shankarāchārya. He wrote commentaries on Upanishads, Bhagavad Gitā and Brahmasutra (collectively known as Prasthāntrayi) and started the *Advait* (monism) school. He travelled all over India and started centers and temples to revive the sagging influence of Hinduism. He wrote several books on the theme that there is only one Truth - God and everything else is illusion (*māyā*). Even though he preached monism and considered man to be a part of God**, he did not have any problem with the prevailing multiplicity of gods. He wrote several hymns in the praise of different deities. Then another scholar Mādhvāchārya came and started the 'Dvaita' (dualism) school. This trend continued

---

*The *mantras* for initiation were: *(1) Buddham sharanam gachhāmi,* (I go unto Buddha), (2) *Sangham sharanam gachhāmi* (I go unto *sangha*), (3) *Dhammam sharanam gachhāmi* (I go unto *dharma*). The word *sangha* means organization but in those days it stood for the Buddhist organization.

** His famous *Nirvāna Khatak* (*Shivoham, Shivoham*) is simply an elaboration of the *Mahāvākya - Aham Brahmāsmi.*

and a succession of *Āchāryas'* * expounded their views of Vedānta that were some modified forms of these two. Each wrote his own commentaries on Prasthāntrayi, which became a prerequisite for starting a new school of thought. The prominent among those who followed were Vallabha, Rāmānuja, and Nimbārk. It is interesting to note that each claimed that the original material in Prasthāntrayi supported his views. The commentaries of these *Āchāryas* are considered classics in *Vedānta* literature.

The Veda Samhitās are the earliest of the Vedic literature. They are collections of hymns sung in the praise of deities mostly representing the forces of nature and describing rituals to perform yajnas to please them. The hymns consist of a number of verses (*shlokas*) and are called *Suktas*. Indra, Varuna, Mitra, Agni are the prominent gods. Indra is the king of all gods, Varuna is the god of water and the bright blue sky. Mitra regulates the course of the Sun; Agni is the Fire God who chose to live among mortals and acts as an intermediary between man and the other gods by receiving oblations and worship for them. Several other names come up in the hymns but their roles and qualities overlap. When we look closely at these gods, it becomes apparent that even though the prayers were mostly for material welfare and happiness, the sages recognized the existence of an indwelling Spirit behind each natural phenomenon. Even at this early stage of development of man's spiritual consciousness the Vedic seers went so far as to realize that there was just one God behind the many gods invoked in their prayers. Behind the apparent multiplicity of gods there is almost everywhere an underlying theme of one God. This is clearly expressed as each god is invoked and worshipped

---

* The days of sages were over. So the learned preachers were called *Āchāryas*. The word denotes a combination of guru and scholar.

as omnipotent, omniscient, and omnipresent. There is ample evidence in the Samhitās that these seers worshipped one and the same Supreme Being in His different manifestations. One of the hymns in Rigveda puts it clearly : "They call Him Indra, Mitra, Varuna and Agni. The Truth is one but sages call Him by different names."* In their search for Truth these seers went further and came to realize God in an impersonal form above and beyond the concept of a cosmic Deity. In describing this Supreme Being they said : "There was neither what is, nor what is not. There was no sky, nor the heaven. Then death was not, nor immortality; there was no difference of day and night. That One breathed, breathless in Itself. It existed but without exerting or manifesting Itself, and there was nothing other than It"** — God before the origin of the universe being described in neuter terms. Thus even in the earliest stages the concept of pure monism was clearly behind the outward manifestation of gods and rituals.

The concept of one God without form and attributes serving as a backdrop for all gods has pervaded throughout the history of Hinduism. However, as far as the names of gods are concerned, there was almost a revolution after the *Vedic* period. The names like Indra, Mitra and Varuna were almost forgotten. Other names like Rudra and Vishnu mentioned in Vedic hymns, became prominent when along with Brahma they came to occupy the top place as the Trinity. They were associated with the three stages of creation, preservation, and dissolution through which the universe has to go through. As discussed earlier, the trinity represents three aspects of the same God who uses *Māyā* or

---

* ---- *ekam sat viprāh bahudhā vadanti.* Rigveda, I, 164-46.

** *Nāsadiya Sukta,* Rigveda, X, 129.

Prakriti to create the universe.* *Prakriti* consists of three *gunas* (primordial modes of energy) and five elements. The three *gunas* are *Sattwa, Rajas* and *Tamas*. Sattwa implies purity and knowledge, Rajas : passion and restless activity, and Tamas : ignorance and indolence. These gunas evolve into ego, mind, senses, bodies, and sense objects. The five elements are earth, water, air, ether or space, and fire.** Getting back to gods then, the creation of gods to represent different aspects of the One was a matter of convenience — to let the common man have a specific image of God. The mode of worship also changed. It became more elaborate with rituals but the *yajnas* of the Vedic period remained as a special feature in every important religious function. The personal god appeared in several forms, male as well as female. The worship of Shakti as the divine power became as prevalent as that of the Trinity. However, in the midst of all this proliferation of gods and goddesses, the Hindu concept of the one Supreme Being and man's urge for spiritual communion with the One remained unchanged. It was recognized by every one, consciously or subconsciously, that God without form and attributes (*nirākār* Brahma) is the background of all the gods that are worshipped. He is the reality behind all the manifested forms in front of the devotee. The manifestations may be different but the unmanifest always remains the same. There are sectarians who might speak of the superiority of their particular gods, incarnations, and prophets, but the true

---

* The word creation here also includes manifestation. When we talk of *Māyā*, the universe is a manifestation; when *Prakriti* is used, it is a creation.

** The significance of the numbers one, three, and five comes from here. Whenever people make donations for a religious cause or give money at an auspicious occasion, they usually add one to the amount (51, 101, etc.). *Mantras* are usually repeated three or five times.

devotees see all gods to be manifestations of some aspect of the One. Whatever be the personal god one starts with, the ultimate goal of the spiritual exercises is to realize the Truth which is one and eternal.

The Vedic hymns praised God and emphasized *yajnas* as a religious practice. This did not satisfy the advanced and intellectually inclined sages who wanted to delve deeper into the nature of God and the universe. This led to a flowering-of-thought period and thus the philosophical parts of Vedās emerged, which were subsequently collected into Upnishads. In a way they resulted from a revolt against the predominantly ritualistic practices of the early Vedic period. Some people got disgusted with the mechanical rituals and began to seek rational solutions of human problems. Thus a new trend emerged, in which meditation rather than performance of rituals became the principal mode of worship. The inner or mental sacrifice as opposed to the outer sacrifice in the form of oblation into the fire became more important and the realization of the Self took center stage. In a chronological sense it can be said that the *samhitās* constitute the first phase of the Vedas, the *Brahmans* the second, the *Āranyaks* the third, and the Upanishads the fourth and the last. The word *Upanishad* derives from the three roots — *up*=near, *ni*=down, *sad*=sit, and so its literal meaning is 'to sit down near someone'. In the Āranyak phase it became a tradition for a son or pupil to sit at the feet of the father or the guru to learn, and the learning process usually involved a dialog between them. It must be remembered, however, that some of the Upanishads are from Brahmans and Samhitās. Therefore the seeds of the philosophy regarding the Self and *Brahma*, that sprouted and flowered in the Upanishads, were there even in the earlier phases.

Vedās and *Purānas* have influenced every facet of Hindu life from time immemorial. Even when we are not performing any religious act, words like Om, Om Tat Sat, Hare Rāma, Hare Krishna etc. come to our lips subconsciously. People use Rāma on every occasion bad or good; they use it for greeting each other, for expressing joy, sorrow, astonishment, and other emotions. Gāyatri Mantra, which is from Rigved, is chanted not only on religious occasions but also routinely as a personal habit. This is the mantra with which a child is initiated into the world of learning. At more advanced stages we use mantras from Upanishads. Hindus have believed in peace from the very beginning. Each Upanishad starts and ends with an invocation of peace and the mantra for this is called *shāntipath*. These mantras are often recited at the end of a religious function or ceremony. One of these is more common and it is the one recited if only one mantra is to be used.* There are famous hymns like *Purusha Sukta, Hiranyagarbha Sukta* and *Devi Sukta* that are used on special occasions. The mantras from Upanishads are used even in other spheres of life. For example, the national motto (*Satyameva Jayate*), appearing on all emblems of the Government of India, comes from one of the major Upanishads**. Educational institutions have also adopted their motto from these mantrās. Those familiar with Banaras Hindu University would recall *Vidyayāmritmashnute* (from *Ishopanishad*) and *Asato Mā Sadgamaya, Tamaso Mā*

---

* Most people understand this mantra as the *shāntipath* because this is the only one that has the word *shānti* at the end of each component part. The full text is given in 'Appendix A'.

** Mundakopanishad, 3.1. 6. The full verse is given in the 'Appendix A'. The minor change in the word *jayati* had to be made because the two words now make a stand-alone sentence. This is related to a subtle aspect of Sanskrit grammar governing verbs.

Jyotirgamaya,   Mrityormāmritam   Gamaya   (from
Brihadāranyak Upnishad). Two of the great sentences *Aham
Brahmāsmi* and *Tat Tvam Asi* are the climax of personal
enlightenment among the students of *Vedas*. In fact
everyone uses something from *Vedas* and *Purānas* at every
phase of life.

The Vedanta literature was disseminated into the West in
the nineteenth century and generated considerable interest
in Europe and America. Some of the most ardent believers
were Max Mueller, Schopenhauer, and Deussen, who
studied Upanishads with as much zeal as any devoted
Vendāntin in India. Schopenhauer called the opening of the
Sanskrit literature to the West 'the greatest gift of our
century ' and prophesied that Indian pantheism (belief that
God and nature are one) might become the popular belief
in the West also. The book Oupnekhat (German translation
of major Upanishads) always lay open on his table. Of this
book he said : "It is the most satisfying and elevating reading
(with the exception of the original text) which is possible in
the world. It has been the solace of my life and will be the
solace of my death." Deussen believed that the thinkers of
the Upanishads obtained "if not the most scientific, yet still
the most intimate and immediate light upon the last secret
of existence" and that in the Upanishads "there are
philosophical conceptions unequalled in India or perhaps
anywhere else in the world." Much later commenting on
the reason for the intensity of Vedanta's appeal to the
western mind, Winternitz said : "These old thinkers wrestle
so earnestly for the truth, and in their philosophical poems
the eternally unsatisfied human yearning for knowledge has
been expressed so fervently. The Upanishads do not contain
superhuman conceptions, but human, absolutely human
attempts to come nearer to the truth — and it is this which
makes them so valuable to us."

The general awareness of Vedanta in the West got another, shot in the arm when Vivekānanda visited the USA and Europe in 1893 - 1895 giving public lectures on Hinduism and India to people who had hitherto seen India only through the colored glasses of writers like Rudyard Kipling and William Foster. He roamed about in foreign lands almost penniless boldly facing opposition and trying to penetrate into the hearts and minds of a few. It was not an easy job and in his own words "he was a much reviled preacher who would not be admitted to a decent hotel". But he was a dauntless spirit and after a sojourn of over two years of hard and persistent labor he was able to collect a number of disciples. Some of them accompanied him back to India and became somewhat of a demonstrable proof of his successful mission abroad. This was probably the first missionary approach in the history of Hinduism, although even here there was no attempt at spreading Hinduism as such. Vivekānanda founded in 1897 a new order of *sanyāsis* - Rāmkrishna Mission for doing philanthropic work along with spreading the teachings of Vedānta. The mission has nearly one hundred centers in India and about half as many in the rest of the world with most of them concentrated in America and Europe.

Following in the footsteps of *Vivekānanda* were others like Rāma Tirth who came to USA via Japan. He also gave lectures on India and Hinduism and developed a small following. This missionary spirit continued on a smaller scale when a few individuals came to the West primarily to teach yoga. It was not until the sixties and seventies that a sizeable number of Hindus started to immigrate to the West and Hinduism got a foothold in the West, especially in the USA and Canada. There had been, of course, immigration of Hindus to Africa, West Indies, Guiānās, and Fiji earlier in the nineteenth century sponsored or forced by the British. But those were mostly laborers and small business communities with little exposure to Vedānta. It must be said to their credit, though, that within their groups they managed to preserve the tradition and culture much better than the later, more intellectually inclined immigrants to the West. It is a different matter that subsequent generations could not hold on to the old values and as a result Hinduism has largely lost its footing in most of those countries. In order for Hinduism to survive abroad, it is imperative that the succeeding generations of Hindu immigrants understand the basic values of the religion and culture and feel proud about them.

CHAPTER TWO

SOCIAL ASPECTS

* * *

The Role of Women

There has been a general misconception, especially in the Western world, that women have a subservient role in Hinduism. This has never been true in the entire history and certainly not in the Vedic and Purānic periods. Women had prominent roles not only in the family and the household but also in the society in general. The very fact that God is also worshipped in female form is indicative of the position of women in the society. When the new bride comes into a family and even later on she is referred to as *Griha Laxmi* (Laxmi of the house). In the Upanishads several women are mentioned who were as learned as men and took part in philosophical discussions. There is the classic example of Gārgi who could argue philosophical points with great sages like Yājnavalkya*. In Rāmāyana Sitā is revered almost as much as Rāma. In Mahābhārata women had dominating

---

* The stories are narrated in the 'Appendix A'.

roles. In the beginning Satyavati as the step- mother of Bhisma dominates the story and later Kunti has a prominent role right to the end. There is also a short story in *Vanaparva* that illustrates the point that a housewife taking care of her family with devotion could have more knowledge than a learned Brāhmin. Much later in the medieval period Mirā became a celebrated saint. In the social and political arena there were women like Laxmi Bāi (Jhānsi Ki Rāni) who became a legend. The society has since seen women like Sarojani Nāidu, Vijaya Laxmi Pandit, and Indira Gandhi make their mark in history. At the religious level even women of non-Indian origin have reached exalted positions. Vivekānanda's disciple Sister Nivedita (Margaret Noble) and 'The Mother' of Arbindo Āshram (Mrs. Richard) are perfect examples.

The discussion above does focus on exceptionally gifted women but it also illustrates the point that Hindu women could achieve greatness and be on par with men right from the dawn of civilization. It does not imply that the women have not been from time to time subjected to injustices. But that happens in every society and Hindus have not been perfect. The *sati* custom was deplorable in the past and the dowry system prevalent in many parts of the country even now is despicable, not to mention its evil consequences like burning of brides. But these are social evils that have nothing to do with the religion. It is not precisely known when and how *sati* custom originated. Some would argue that it originated with Sati, Shiva's wife burning herself with sheer will-power (*tej bal*) when her father Prajāpati Daksha insulted Shiva. The custom became prevalent shortly after the country was overrun by the Muslim conquerors. There is almost no mention of this custom in the Vedic period. In Mahābhārata we do have Pāndu's second wife Mādri becoming *sati* but that was because of the remorse she felt, having been the indirect cause of his death. Whatever its origin and the reason for becoming common place, it was a blot on the society. It must, however, be said that the society did realize this and produced reformers like Rāma Mohan Roy who revolted against the custom and succeeded in eradicating it.

The Caste System : We briefly discussed the caste system in the first part of the book. Here we take a look at how the system originated and to what extent a person's worth depended on the circumstances of his birth. There is a verse in Bhagavad Gitā in which Krishna says: "The four-caste system was created by me for division of work according to the inherent nature *(guna)* of the person" (B.G. 4. 13). If we take this as the starting point, the origin of the system was a pragmatic approach to organize the economic structure of the society. We come across many examples in the Upanishads where men of low birth possess the highest knowledge and highly learned Brāhmins go to them for instructions; the Brāhmins were not exclusive repositories of knowledge. Many of the venerable sages were not Brāhmins. The Kshatriya caste, that constituted the kings and warriors, was closely connected with the intellectual life and literary activities in the vedic period. King Janak is a shining example, who often confounded priests and sages with his knowledge. We have already referred to Dharmavyādh, the pious hunter and meat-seller, to whom the learned Kaushik Brāhmin went for instructions about philosophy and morality, especially about the theory that it is not birth but virtuous life that makes one Brāhmin. Again the ascetic Jājali finds a teacher in the lowly merchant Tulādhār. Then there is the story of Satyakām Jābala of questionable parentage who is lauded and accepted as a pupil by sage Gautam.* Much later, when the caste system had degenerated into an evil custom, we find people of the lowest class like Narsimha Bhagat and Raidās respected as saints.

The original concept of division of labor was in conformity with the laws of nature as it also took into account the inherent abilities *(gunas)* of the individual. The choice of the word caste might have been unfortunate; in reality it represented class in as much as it was not tied to birth. Even with equal opportunities all human beings can not attain the same level in life. A classless society is a utopia in that sense. Stratification is a phenomenon of nature, it can not be done away with. All that a just and rational society can do is to create conditions that let everyone realize his full potential irrespective of the circumstances of his birth. After that it is up to the individual to attain his level and that can not be dictated by external forces. Actions of the society or the government can be helpful only to a point; pushed beyond that point they can be detrimental instead.

This is, of course, one side of the caste system. The diehards among the proponents of the system would argue that the castes and their duties had been defined as early as in Rigved *(Purusha Sukta).* But the fact is that in the days of the *Smritis* the priest class saw in the caste system the most effective way to make their position in the society safe and secure. Thus the new scriptures elaborated on the theme of superiority of the upper classes. They went to the extent of denying not only the lowest class *(shudras)* but also women and some business classes the right to study Vedas (*stree shudra dvij bandhunām, trayi na shruti gocharāh* — Shrimad Bhāgavatam). The system was made rigid and the caste became a permanent fixture with the family and its

---

* *Chhandogya Upanishad*, IV-4. The story is narrated in 'Appendix A'.

descendents. The word untouchable became associated with the lowest classes that came to be treated as sub-human. It was against this background that reform movements like Jainism and Buddhism sprang up. Buddha's following, in particular, grew rapidly because he put stress on human dignity. His concept of *dhamma* (dharma in Sanskrit) was nothing more than 'having few faults and many good habits like mercy, charity, truthfulness, and purity'. There was nothing new here but the ritualistic Hindu society had moved away from these basics. Buddhism did not come to be regarded as a separate religion until much later. Emperor Ashoka, who was responsible more than anyone else for the spread of Buddhism in India and abroad, never considered it other than a reformist trend in Hinduism. Towards the end of his reign the caste system had weakened and lost its rigidity. People from every caste were doing every type of work and this trend continued for several centuries after Ashoka. When Buddhism came to be regarded as a separate religion, especially after its break up into two branches — *Mahāyān* and *Hinyān*, it became almost extinct in India. The orthodox Hinduism again took hold and unfortunately the caste system became prevalent again; in some parts of India it got much worse than before. The constant changes in the political landscape of the country and its fragmentation did not allow any reformist movement to take hold for a millenium. It was only in the nineteenth century, when the country became one under the British rule, that the reformist zeal surfaced again. Later it was Gandhi who tried to glorify the low caste Hindus by calling them *Harijans* (God's people) and starting a countrywide movement to give them a respectable place in the general community. People like Dr. Ambedkar started a reform movement from within the backward classes and made their plight a political issue. They were classified as scheduled classes or tribes and were given special privileges in education and employment opportunities. After independence the attempts to redress the wrongs were extended to a broader class. The rigidity of the system has now almost vanished largely because of the spread of education and in most urban areas it is non-existent for all practical purposes. Now the word *Harijan* has almost disappeared and *dalit* (trampled) seems to be in vogue.

Rebirth

One of the basic beliefs in Hinduism is that of rebirth and the transmigration of soul. This belief, in turn, comes from the fundamental doctrines of the Upanishads embodied in the two words Brāhman (or Brahm) and *Ātmā.* (Self). The entire discussion of the Upanishads revolves around these two words and their inter-relationship. One of the four so-called great sentences (*Mahāvākyas*) of Vedanta is 'This ātmā is Brāhman' *(ayam ātmā Brahm* - Brihadāranyak Upanishad*).* It sums up the relationship between the individual soul and God : the soul is an infinitesimal part of the infinite that is God. The soul therefore is indestructible, it does not die with the physical body. Realizing the Self is realizing God. The fortunes of the individual soul are tied with the action of the person. When the soul departs from the body upon death, it carries the imprint of the person's actions (*karma*) and the consequences of the actions of the previous life remain with it. The soul wanders in the Beyond and once it finds the opportunity for a suitable abode, it enters into a new body and starts all over again. If the good actions keep accumulating, the soul becomes pure and merges with the Infinite. Until it reaches that perfection, it keeps going through the cycle of birth and death. As summed up in Brihadāranyak Upanishad, 'Man is formed entirely out of desire, and according to his desire is his resolve, and according to his resolve he performs actions, and according to his actions is his destiny'. This doctrine is the starting point of the moral element and ethics in Hinduism, even though in the Upanishads there is hardly any moral teaching as such. As mentioned earlier, there are no commandments in Vedānta. The doctrine of karma has pervaded through Hinduism from the very beginning and plays through the consciousness of every Hindu.

Much has been written about rebirth and transmigration of soul. Numerous instances of people remembering the details of the previous life have been reported in every part of the world, so the concept is not unique to Hinduism. Questions like : 'Where have we come from?', 'Where do we go?', 'What after death?' have been asked in every society and culture. Every religion accepts the basic premise of the karma theory that good deeds make a person better. Vedānta philosophy carries the concept further beyond death and before birth. It goes beyond the confines of human experience and tries to answer the above questions in a rational way. It identifies nature and everything else in it with God. Everything in nature is transient although the difference in the time scales may make us think otherwise. Every thing, living or otherwise, seemingly appears from nowhere and disappears into nowhere. Human beings are subject to the same rule. A person comes from the unmanifest at birth and goes back into it after death, having a brief manifested existence in between. So death is, as if, the permanent state of existence and life is just a perturbation. It is only during the brief manifest period that the person has a chance to change his state through performance of actions. Taking an analogy from physical sciences we may consider the state of existence between death and birth as the ground state of an atom or a molecule and the life as an excited state. Whether the person returns to a higher or lower state after next death depends how much he has added to or subtracted from his initial state through the actions performed in this life. If his normal state keeps going up, he eventually reaches the highest state and merges with God. Again this mode of thinking is not unique to Hinduism. Even Western thinkers lend support for such ideas. To quote Carl Jung : "Life is an energy process. Like every energy process it is, in principle, irreversible and is therefore unequivocally directed towards a goal. That goal is a state of rest. In the long run everything that happens is, as it were, nothing more than the initial disturbance of a perpetual state of rest which forever attempts to re-establish itself."

★ ★ ★

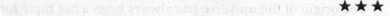

CHAPTER THREE

HINDUISM AND COSMOLOGY

The origin of the universe has always been a hot topic for discussion and investigation in theology as well as science. In Hinduism this has been discussed from the very beginning. The earliest mention of the origin of the cosmos is in Rigved in Hiranyagarbh Sukta, according to which the first thing to appear was a golden egg floating in the vast ocean (which must have been created first) and everything else originated from this egg. Later the origin is discussed in the Upanishads in greater detail. In the beginning there was only God. He desired to become many or create objects and beings and created the things one by one. Since every thing originated from Him, the Universe is a manifestation rather than creation. That is why in the view of Vedānta every thing is God. According to the Advait philosophy God is the only reality, everything else is illusion (*Brahm satyam jagat mithyā* - Shankarāchārya in Vivekchudamani). The universe originates from God and at the end it goes back into Him. The view of Sānkhya philosophy is slightly different, according to which the Universe is created by an interaction between Purusha and Prakriti and the two are independent. The Vedānta view is that Prakriti originates from Purusha (Brahman) and is not independent. Even within Vedanta there is the Dvaita school according to which the world is created by God but it is real and not illusory. But the general concept still includes the notion that everything originated from God : "As a spider spins out her web out of herself, as out of a fire the little sparks fly in all directions, so out of God emanate all worlds, all gods, and all beings."

Why God wanted to become many or create is a question that may never be answered. However, there are possible explanations. These are just conjectures and certainly open to discussion and critical examination. We have to keep in mind that, although we use the word creation, we actually mean manifestation. The tendency to express the self is probably inherent to all objects animate or inanimate. A bud blooms into a flower. A seed sprouts, becomes a tree, flowers, bears fruits and ultimately returns to the seed form. An artist expresses himself in the art he creates. Any physical entity with creative ability must strive for self-expression. This is, in a way, hinted at in Svetāshvatar Upanishad (6.1). God being the ultimate and only source for everything has the same tendency. So the desire to become many or to create *lokas* reflects the urge for self-expression. From this point of view the question as to why God created the universe becomes moot.

Another way of looking at the issue is to consider the manifestation process as that of expansion and contraction. Since the universe originates from God (and merges into Him at dissolution), it is already in Him in latent form. Just as the tree is contained in the tiny seed and its various stages of growth unfold under proper conditions, the various stages of evolution of the universe emanate from God. One can imagine that 'proper conditions' prompted Him to desire to become many.

The most abstract concept of God is that God is a state of existence — the highest possible state. There is a corresponding lowest state and many states in between. Everything in the universe exists in one of these states. If all the states are taken as a unit, one can imagine that all have collapsed into one composite state. So when Upanishads say that in the beginning there was only one *Sat*, it is equivalent to saying that there was only one state of existence. This view is consistent with the description of *lokas* in Brihadāranyak Upanishad (3.6). Each loka or sphere may be regarded as a state, *Brahmaloka* being the highest and *Pātāl loka* being the lowest. As Yājnavalkya replied to Gārgi's questions, each is contained in the next higher one until we get to the highest, so all are contained in Brahmaloka. Her last question - "What is Brahmaloka contained in?" was tantamount to asking — "What is the origin of Brahma?" There is no answer to that question.

It is interesting to note that modern cosmology also has the same problem. The generally accepted big bang theory can get to the instant of explosion but very little is known about the precise nature of the universe at the initial moment (space - time singularity). The discussions of open and closed universe lead to the conclusion that the expanding universe will ultimately reverse its trend and start contracting, finally collapsing into the singularity. The time scales involved are not very different (at least qualitatively) from those described in ancient Hindu literature (for example, Mahābhārata, Shanti Parva 231.12-31); according to these calculations one *'kalpa'*, i.e. one half day of *Brahmadev* is about 4.32 billion years. The life span of the Universe is one day.

★ ★ ★

CHAPTER FOUR

EPICS AND MODERN TECHNOLOGY

The Epics, Rāmāyana and Mahābhārata, represent the essence of Hinduism in as much as they strive to summarize the teachings of the Vedas and Purānas. Both contain descriptions of superhuman feats that could be taken only on faith because they were beyond the realm of human experience and there was no rational explanation for them. But human experience is not static, it is changing constantly. Half a century ago no one would have believed that man could walk on the moon or space travel was possible. The same is true in almost any field of science and technology. Looking back from that perspective we begin to wonder if the things described in the Epics were for real. Although some of them still seem beyond belief, they might not be so after a few decades. We examine a few of the supernatural phenomena of the Epics in the light of the successes achieved by modern technology.

Rāmāyana : One of the well-known futuristic conceptions in this Epic was the airplane - *Pushpak Vimān*. No one in the contemporary world had even thought of such a thing. How did Vālmiki conceive of the machine? We will perhaps never know. But he did and described not just a machine that could fly but something equivalent to the present day jumbo jets that could transport the entire army across the country. True, we do not have any details of how it worked but the very fact that the sage was able to describe its flight and the scenes on the ground below is beyond comprehension. Pushpak was supposedly made available to Rāma by the gods. But even earlier in the story, when Rāvana abducted Sitā, he also used some sort of an air vehicle to take her to Lankā.

Another incredible thing that we come across in Rāmāyana is Hanumān being able to jump across land and sea covering hundreds of miles. In search of Sitā he jumps across the sea to Lankā; when Laxman is seriously wounded, he flies across the country to bring a herb from the Himalayas and not able to locate the exact spot of the herb he brings a piece of the mountain. On the way back he is shot down by Bharat and then promptly put back in the orbit by another arrow. These were superhuman feats. But in this age of rockets, when huge loads can be put into orbit with precision, they can be accorded some plausibility. Did people in those ancient days possess some techniques to accomplish something equivalent to the rocket function?

Mahābhārata : This Epic by Vyās is more comprehensive and voluminous. It covers a vast range of human emotions and experiences. Since the main theme of this Epic is the war between forces of evil and good represented by Kauravas and Pāndavas, the emphasis is more on personal skills with weapons. The most versatile and potent weapon of the times was the arrow and the individual skill was far more important than the armory. The celebrated heroes were those with the highest level of proficiency with arrows. One of the stringent tests was in Draupadi's *swayamvar* *, where the aspirants had to hit the eye of a rotating fish several feet above ground by looking at the reflection in oil contained in a flat basin on the ground. Only two persons, Arjuna and Karna were capable of accomplishing such a feat. *Arjuna* did it and won Draupadi as Karna was disqualified because of his parentage. This was something extremely difficult but not superhuman. But the skills used during the war did seem incredible. Arrows were used to hit targets miles away and not in the line of sight. One of the most complicated maneuvers made by an arrow was during the slaying of Jayadrath. His father had obtained a boon from gods that his son would not die unless discarded by the father himself. When Jayadrath's head was severed by Arjuna's arrow, his father was sitting in meditation miles away from the battleground. The arrow carried the head on its tip and dropped it on the open palms of his father. With his eyes closed in meditation he thought that some filthy object had fallen on his hands and he dropped the head to the ground in disgust, so the son died. Such a feat by an arrow was incredible. Even in the modern technological warfare such precision targeting could not have been thought of a few decades ago. With the present guided missile technology it is possible, although not with the precision required in the cited story. Again we start thinking if the warriors in those days possessed skills that could make arrows function like guided missiles.

During the battle arrows were not only hurled at the

---

* Strictly speaking this was not a *swayamvar* nor was it so in the case of *Sitā swayamvar* in Rāmāyana. *Swayamvar* implies that the girl is free to choose the groom. In both these cases the choice was conditioned upon the aspirant meeting a certain condition using his power or skill.

enemy but were used as frequently as defensive weapons to cut down the incoming enemy arrows. This again required tremendous skill and concentration. In the light of modern technology this function of the arrows reminds us of the defensive missiles intended for intercepting incoming missiles. Then there is the incredible story of Arjun weaving a pattern of arrows to make a reasonably comfortable deathbed for Bhishma as he fell mortally wounded. Bhishma could choose the time of his death and lay there until the sun became northbound. There is nothing in modern technology with which to compare these achievements but how can one deny the possibility of such things happening in the future?

It is quite likely that there was something more than just physical power or skill involved in all these incredible feats. In the scriptures we often come across descriptions of things accomplished by sheer will power (*man-shakti* or *manobal*). The gods were endowed with such power and they could create things just by projecting an intense desire. We have an example of this in the birth of Ganesh when Pārvati creates the boy out of discarded saffron flakes. This can be regarded simply as an extension of God's power to create by will, since all gods and goddesses are manifestations of certain aspects of the same God. Some of the great sages and yogis were also·endowed with such power. Modern science has just now begun to delve into these mysteries and the subject of mind-body interaction has become a topic of serious investigation. Perhaps an intense willpower combined with the extraordinary skills made those supernatural feats possible. A century later or sometime into the future, the same feats may not seem supernatural or incredible. Time will tell.

APPENDIX A

GEMS FROM THE SCRIPTURES

We give here some excerpts from the religious literature, whose applicability transcends time and space. Some are anecdotes that have been referred to in the text, others are presented as examples of the versatility of the topics and their significance in day to day life. The transliteration of the original texts is provided for the sake of completeness.

FROM UPNISHADS :
Gārgi (Brihadāranyak Upanishad 3. 6)

Gārgi Vāchaknavi (daughter of Vāchaknu) was one of most learned women of the *Vedic* period. She could hold her own in any philosophical discussion with any contemporary sage. Once, King Janak organized a special *yajna (bahudakshinā yajna)* in which all the prominent sages and learned priests of the nation participated. After the completion of the *yajna*, Janak offered one thousand cows with ten gold coins tied to their horns to the Brahmin among them who had the knowledge of Brahma (*Brahmanishtha* among those sages and priests). No one dared to claim that knowledge. The venerable Yāgyavalkya was also among them. He looked around and then told his disciple Somashravā to take the cows. The other Brāhmins got angry and asked him how he claimed himself to be a *Brahmanishtha*.

"I salute the *Brahmanishtha*, I only aspire to be one. But I am desirous of the cows." The sage said calmly.

"Do you know the *Sutra* and the knowledge of Brahma

that it leads to?'' Another prominent sage Uddālak asked.
"Yes, I know.''

"Any one can say — 'I know, I know'. If you know, then explain. And if you will not be able to explain, your head will fall off.''

One by one the sages and priests asked him questions and Yāgyavalkya answered. In the Upanishad one sub-chapter is devoted to one questioner and one topic. At the end he asked them six questions, they could not answer any, and he had the cows taken away to his *āshram*.

One of the questioners was Gārgi. She started with the question:

"All the things that we see around us, what are they contained in?''

"They are all contained in water.''

"What is water contained in?''

"In air.''

"What is air contained in?''

"In space.''

"What is space contained in?''

"In *Gandharva loka*.''

Thus each time he answered her question, she turned the answer around into another question and he kept on answering patiently. Finally he mentioned *Brahmaloka* and she asked :

"What is *Brahmaloka* contained in?''

"*Gārgi*, you are asking a super- question (ati*prashna*) that should never be asked. You are asking this question about One who should not be questioned. Don't ask this question, lest your head fall off : '*Gārgi mātiprokshirmā te moordhā byapaptadanatiprashnyam vai devatāmatiprichhasi. Gārgi mātiprakshiditi.*''

Gārgi then became silent. The point here is that she could take the discussion to the highest possible level beyond which no one had answers.

In this story (as well as in other places) there is reference to 'the head falling off'. The symbolism of this may have several subjective interpretations. Here is what I prefer. The reasoning and logical questioning can go only to a point. If one persists in going beyond that point, one is bound to fall into an abyss from which there would be no return. On the other hand if one lets his ego *(ahamkār)* become introvert and all pervasive, he is bound to fall into a deep sea of ignorance. One question is *atiprashna*, the other is *jalpa*, i.e. questions and arguments not for gaining knowledge but testing someone. This is what Uddālak was doing when he asked Yāgyavalkya to answer their questions. In either case the person indulging in such questions is courting intellectual death.

Satyakām *(Chhāndogya Upanishad 4. 4)*

There was a boy named Satyakām who grew up in sages *ashrams* as his mother Jabalā worked as maid servant in there. Having grown among the sages and their students, he also wanted to study. When he came to the proper age his mother's permission went to Sage Gautam and requested to be admitted in the *ashram* as a pupil. The sage asked what was his *gotra* as that was the information he needed to find out the boy's lineage.

"I don't know Sir, I will go and ask my mother".

Coming back home he asked mother, what was his *gotra* ?

She said to him "I don't know son. In my youth I had to move about much while waiting on the guests in the *ashrams* and I conceived you during that period. So I don't know what family you belong to. I am Jabalā by name and you are Satyakām. So you are Satyakām Jābal and tell your guru so."

The boy went back to the Sage and told him exactly what the mother had told. The Sage was highly impressed by the innate truthfulness of the boy. He said to him:

"No one but a true Brahmin would speak out thus *(naitad brāhmano vivattamarhati)*. Go and fetch fuel, I will initiate you. You have not swerved from the path of truth."

The story is yet another example how loosely the caste system was tied to birth in the ancient times.

Yāgyavalkya - Maitreyi Conversation (Brihadaranakya Upanishad 2. 4)

Yāgyavalkya decided to take *sanyās* and leave the *ashram*. He wished to settle things for his two wives before leaving. He gave the proper share to the first wife and then told the second wife Maitreyi to take the rest. Maitreyi asked him:

"Should all this wealth, even the whole world belong to me, will I become immortal?"

"No, you can enjoy all the material happiness which the riches can bring, but wealth can not give you immortality."

Maitreyi said "What shall I do with all this which can not give me immortality? What my lord knows (of immortality) tell that to me (*yenāham namritāsyām kimaham ten kuryām. Yadev bhagavān ved, tadev me bruhiti*)."

Yāgyavalkya then replied "You are truly dear to me, you speak dear words. Come, sit down and I will explain to you; listen well to what I say." And he started with explaining why things are dear to one.

"A husband is not dear for the sake of the husband (that you may love the husband), he is dear for the sake of the Self" (*Na vā are patyuh kāmaya pati priyo bhavati, ātmanastu kāmāya pati priyo bhavati*).

"A wife is not dear for the sake of the wife, she is dear for the sake of the Self." (*Na vā are jāyāyai kāmāya jāyā priyā bhavati, ātmanastu kamaya jāyā priyā bhavati*).

"Children are not dear for the sake of children, they are dear for the sake of the Self." (*Na vā are putrānām kāmāya putrāh priya bhavanti, ātmanastu kāmāya putrāh priya bhavanti*).

"Money is not dear for the sake of money, it is dear for the sake of Self." (*Na vā are vittasya kāmāya vittam priyam bhavati, ātmanastu kāmāya vittam priyam bhavati).*

And so on he goes talking about all the things that are dear to one. At the end he says:

"Therefore, it is well-known in this world that it is only the Self that is dear, nothing else." *(Tasmāt lokprasiddhametal - ātmeva priyah nānyat).*

This is regarded as one of the most famous passages in the Upanishads. The philosophy is very abstract but we can see its significance in practical life. For one thing, it teaches us to love everyone and every thing close to us as our own self. It also helps us to keep a balanced view of relationships both in prosperity and adversity. We often hear religious discourses about attachment and the need for detachment. In order to shed attachment we need to understand the nature of our attachment with people and things. And that is what this conversation is all about. Starting with the closest family, we love husband, wife, or children because they are our own. The Self is the soul and there is a close affinity of the souls. When two people get married they pledge to consider their two bodies and souls one and loving each other is nothing but loving the Self. The child is born to parents because the soul wandering about in the invisible finds compatibility and affinity with the two souls of the parents. Thus the soul in the child is also a reflection of the Self. The same is true for friends, we do not become friends haphazardly; we become friends only when the natures and habits are compatible. This is nothing but compatibility of the souls. The same idea can be carried over to our love for God, which leads to the affinity of the soul with the Supreme Reality. With material things the nature of attachment is slightly different, still it leads to the Self. Very few people love money just to look at it, they love it because it is capable of providing material comforts to them and those dear to them. Detachment does not mean forgetting these affinities and relationships but understanding their true nature.

A Historic Quotation (Shvetāshvatar Upanishad)

Swami Vivekānanda's address at the World Parliament of Religions in Chicago in September 1893 was a remarkable event in the annals of Hinduism. In fact he gave five lectures at the Parliament on September 11, 15, 19, 20 and 27; the main address on Hinduism and Vedānta was on the nineteenth. In this address he referred to and quoted from two verses from Shvetāshvatar Upanishad taking a piece from one (Children of Immortal Bliss) and almost the entire text from the other. As a historical note we give here the relevant part of his speech and the two verses.

  "......, Hear, ye children of immortal bliss! I have found the Ancient One who is beyond all darkness, all delusion; knowing Him alone you shall be saved from death over again". "Children of immortal bliss" — what a hopeful name! Allow me to call you, brethren, by that sweet name - heirs of immortal bliss. Ye, the Hindu refuses to call you sinners. We are the Children of God, the sharers of immortal bliss, holy perfect beings. Ye divinities on earth — sinners! It is a sin to call a man so; it is a standing libel on human nature....."

Hear, 'ye children of immortal bliss' is the translation of *'shrinvantu vishwe amritasya putrā'* in :

  Yuje vām brahm purvyam namobhih, vishlok etu pathveva sūreh

  Shrinvantu vishwe amritasya putrā, ā ye dhāmāni divyāni tasthuh. (*Shvet. Up.* 2. 5; also *Rigveda* 10. 13-1)

(O mind and intellect, *) I salute the source of all universe - the Omniscient God, who is the controller of you both, and taking shelter unto Him I unite with Him. These verses of mine describing the glory of God may spread to the entire world like the fame of a great learned person and be heard with apt attention by all children of the immortal One, including those who are in the celestial abodes.

---

* This is the context from the previous verse.

Vedāhmeṭam purusham mahāntam,
āditya varnam tamasah parastāt
Tameva viditwāti mrityumeti,
nānyah panthā vidyateyanāya.
(Shvet. Up. 3. 8; also Yajurrveda 31. 18)

I know that greatest of the great Being Who is beyond darkness and self-effulgent like the sun. Only by knowing Him one can get out of the birth and death cycle, there is no other way.

The Mahāvākyas

The four so-called *Mahāvākyas* (great sentences) of *Vedānta* are also from the Upanishads. These are: (1) *Tat tvam asi* (you are that) from Chhāndogya, (2) *Aham Brahmāsmi* (I am Brahm) from Brihadārnyak, (3) *Ayam ātmā Brahm* (This *Ātmā* is Brahm) from Brihadāranyak, and (4) *Pragyānam Brahm* (Brahm is consciousness) from Aitareya. It is not possible or even necessary, to discuss all of these sentences in detail here. The first one is associated with an interesting story and that is the one presented here.

Uddālak Āruni was a famous sage. When his son *Shvetketu* completed twelve years of age he told him to go to a teacher and learn all that is to be learnt, as in his family it was a tradition not to be Brahmin in name only but also in terms of knowledge. The son then went away for studies and returned home after twelve years. Having learnt all that he could, he was very proud to the point of being arrogant, as now he considered himself to be a truly learned man. One day his father called him and said:

"Shvetketu, now that you regard yourself learned, tell me something. Did you learn the principle by which that which is unheard becomes heard, un-thought becomes thought, and unknown becomes known?"

"No, Sir, my honorable teachers did not tell me of this. They also did not know because if they did, they would have surely taught me that. Please tell me about it."

The father then proceeded to explain the oneness of the entire creation. There was only One in the beginning without a second and everything we see and perceive came out of Him. He has entered into everything and in the living beings He is the soul. Therefore the soul—the Self is Him. At the end everything goes back into Him. His existence is eternal with no beginning, no end and therefore He is infinite. But He is also minute when existing in every being and that minute thing is Ātman.

"Therefore, O Shvetketu, thou are That."

"Explain to me further, father."

"Very well, bring me a fruit from the banyan tree over there."

Shvetketu brought the tiny fruit and the father asked him to split it.

He did.

"What do you see there in?"

"Very tiny seeds."

"Take one and split it."

He split the seed and the father again asked him, "what do you see in the seed ?"

The son said, he saw nothing.

"My dear Shvetketu, what you call nothing contains in it that huge banyan tree. In the same way the very minute thing that constitutes all beings, is the Ātman, and thou are That."

Shvetketu was still bewildered and asked him to explain further.

"Very well. Place this piece of salt into the jug of water and come back to me tomorrow morning."

When Shvetketu came back in the morning, the father asked him to bring the salt that he gave him the day before. He could not get it because the salt had become one with the water.

"Can you see it?"

"No, Sir."

"Can you taste it?"

"Yes, Sir."

He asked him to taste it taking the water from different sides but it tasted the same.

"My dear son, just as you can not see the salt in the water, that One residing within you is not seen but He is there. And He in the form of that minute thing, which is Ātman, is you. Thou are That *Shvetketu.*"

Satyameva Jayate (Mundak Upnishad 3. 1. 6)

Satyameva jayati nānritam,
satyen panthā vitato devayānah
Yenākramanti rishiyo hyāptakāmā,
yatra tat satyasya paramam nidhānam.

Only truth comes out victorious, not falsehood, because the path called *devayān* (the path of gods) is pervaded by truth. Where the eternally satisfied sages roam, that is the permanent abode of the ultimate truth, God.

As mentioned in the text, the change of the word *jayati* into *jayate* was to meet some subtle requirements of Sanskrit grammar governing verbs. It has to do with the difference between *ātmane pad* and *parasmai pad* of the verb.

Shāntipāth

Om Dyau shāntih, antariksham shāntih, prithvi shāntih, āpo shāntih, aushadhiyah shāntih, vanaspatayah shāntih, vishvedevāh shāntih, brahm shāntih, sarvam shāntih, shāntireva shāntih, sā mā shāntiredhi. Om shāntih, shāntih, shāntih.

Om, may there be peace in the sky, may there be peace in the space, may there be peace on earth, may there be peace in water, may there be peace in the herbal plants, may the trees be in peace, may there be peace with the gods, may Brahma be at peace, may all be at peace. May that peace, real peace be mine. *Om*, peace, peace, peace.

From Rāmāyana

When Rāma, with his make-shift army, is poised to attack Rāvana, his younger brother *Vibheeshan* tries to counsel him to return Sitā and make peace with Rāma. But *Rāvana* abuses him. At the end *Vibheeshan* says :

Sulabhāh purushā rājan, satatam priyavādinah
Priyasya cha pathyasya, vaktā shrotā cha durlabhah.

(*Yuddha Kānd* 16. 21)

O king, abundant are people who will always tell what is pleasing to you. But rare are those who will say or hear what is healthy though very unpleasant.

After Rāvana is killed and Sitā regained, Rāma makes her go through the fire-test (*agni pareekshā*) to prove her purity. These are the two famous verses spoken by Sitā before entering the fire.

Yathā me hridayam nityam nāpasarpati Raghavāt
Tatha lokasya sākshe mām sarvatah pātu pāvakah.
Yathā mām shuddha chāritrām dushtām jānāti Rāghavah
Tatha lokasya sākshe mām sarvatah pātu pāvakah.

(*Yuddha Kānd* 116. 25-26)

As my heart has been constantly pervaded by *Rāghava*, so may the fire, who is the ultimate witness of all and everything, engulf me in his protection.

As I, of pure conduct is being considered a fallen woman by Rāghava, so may the fire, who is the ultimate witness of all and everything, engulf me in his protection.

From Mahabhārat
Story of Dharmavyādha

Mahābhārata is replete with sub-stories that convey subtle points of Vedānta philosophy. This story is from *Vanaparva*. There was a young Kaushik brāhmin who had studied the scriptures and practiced yoga from a very young age and had acquired extraordinary powers. One day he was meditating under a tree. There was a small bird sitting on a branch directly above him and happened to answer the call of nature. The droppings fell on the brāhmin who got disgusted and angry. He looked up in anger and the bird was burnt alive. He then proceeded to the river to wash himself again; after that he went into the nearby village to obtain food in alms, as was the practice in those days. He came to the first house and asked for food in his loud voice. There was no response so he repeated his request again and waited. The woman of the house took a long time in getting him the food and he got irritated and then angry. He asked her why she had made him wait so long.

She said : "My husband had come home after hard work and I was busy taking care of him, that is why I got delayed. I am sorry."

This made him still angrier; to him it seemed to be an insult that she considered him less important than the husband. He even threatened her of ill consequences. She calmly told him not to be angry but he would not be pacified. Then she said:

"O, Brahmin, I am not that little bird, so shed your anger. I know that you burnt that bird with your anger. But anger is the greatest enemy of man, you should know that."

The young brāhmin was stunned, his anger precipitated and turned into humility. How did she know about the bird, she was nowhere around. Then he realized that she must be extremely learned, better than him, and requested her to be his teacher and impart some of her knowledge. She replied that she did not consider herself learned enough but he could go to a nearby town where a hunter named Dharmavyādha lived and who could instruct him in matters of *dharma.*

He never expected a lowly hunter to be capable of teaching anything and his hesitation showed on his face.

The woman said :

"O learned Brahmin, *dharma* can not be learnt and knowledge can not be acquired through logic. This is my considered opinion."

Reluctantly he thanked the woman and started for the town where the hunter lived. When he reached the place, he found him cutting and selling meat. In spite of his disgust for the man's profession he told him how he had been sent to learn *dharma* from him. The hunter told him to come after his shop hours. Then followed a long discourse lasting for several days. The *vyādh* told him that he had aged parents who had to be taken care of and he had adopted the family profession for earning the livelihood. One's profession had nothing to do with his conduct. He knew of the young man's aversion for killing and selling meat. So he first talked about non-violence.

"Non-violence is a supreme objective but it is not religion. We eat grains, drink water, breathe air. All of these have tiny invisible living creatures in them. What do you say about that? You walk along roads, there are innumerable insects that get trampled and killed. What do you say to that? O venerable brahmin, who does not kill in this world? After thinking long and hard I have come to the conclusion that there is no one who is a perfect practitioner of non-violence."

After that Dharmavyādha instructed him on morals and other esoteric aspects of dharma for several days and the Kaushik Brahmin acquired great knowledge and also humility.

Again the moral of this story is that the greatness of a man is not determined by how and where he is born but by his conduct. A profession in itself is not bad if it is carried out of necessity. How a person conducts himself in his daily life is more important.

Yudhishthir - Yaksha *Conversation*

This story is also from *Vanaparva*. When the Pāndavas were roaming about in forests in exile, one day all five brothers went to explore the new place. Walking along they stopped for rest. All of them were thirsty and Yudhishthir asked the youngest one to look for water. Sahadeva went in search of water and found a clean pond with clear water. He decided to drink water before taking it to the brothers. As soon as he tried to dip his hands into the water, he heard a clear voice :

"Before you drink water you have to answer my questions."

Sahadeva looked around and saw no one and again tried to drink but the voice warned again. He ignored the warning and proceeded to drink but before he could get water to his mouth he fell unconscious. When he did not return, Yudhishthir sent the next one to look for him.

Nakul found Sahadeva unconscious but before doing anything else he wanted to drink water. The warning voice came again and he ignored it with the same consequence.

One by one Arjuna and Bhima also came. They were more arrogant but met the same fate.

Finally Yudhishthir came and found all four lying unconscious and he immediately sensed that there was something wrong. He proceeded to the edge of the pond cautiously and as he got nearer the voice came again : "I am the *Yaksha* in-charge of this pond. Your brothers ignored my warning and met their fate. If you don't want to end up like them, answer my questions first and then drink."

Yudhishthir agreed and told the unseen *Yaksha* to ask the questions. He answered the questions one by one.

The first set of questions was :

"Who carries greater weight than earth and who is higher than sky? Who is faster than wind and what is more numerous than straws?"

"Mother has greater weight than earth, father is higher than sky, mind is faster than wind, and anxiety is more numerous than straws. "

Then he asked several other questions and Yudhishthir gave satisfactory answers. One of these questions was: "How does a man attain the status of a brāhmin, by birth, education, studying scriptures, or by his conduct?"

"O venerable *Yaksha*, one does not become brāhmin by birth, education, or learning. There is no doubt that he becomes brāhmin only by his conduct."

A part of another question was: "What is the most surprising thing and what is the right path to follow?"

"Every day people die but the rest want to remain here permanently. What can be more surprising than that ? As to the righteous path, it is well known that logic can not lead us anywhere, the scriptures also say different things, and the words of no one sage can be taken as gospel. If we delve into *dharma*, it is very difficult to reach a conclusion. So the best way to find the right path is to follow in the footsteps of great men."

The latter is again one of the famous verses, so we transliterate the original.

Tarkopratishthah shrutayo vibhinna, naiko rishiryasya matam pramānam

Dharmasya tatwam nihitam guhāyām, mahājano yen gatah sapanthāh. (*Āranya Parva* 313. 117)

The *Yaksha* was satisfied and he appeared now in person. Yudhishthir saluted and asked him to bring the brothers to life before drinking water. The *Yaksha* said that he could bring only one of them to life and Yudhishthir could make his choice. Yudhishthir asked for Sahadeva.

"Why are you wanting Sahadeva when Arjuna or Bhima can be more helpful to you in your attempt to regain your kingdom?"

"We are five brothers from two mothers. Of Kunti's sons I am alive, so I want one of Mādri's sons to be alive."

The Yaksha tried to convince him otherwise but Yudhishthir did not budge. He said :

"Dharma kills those who kill it and it protects those who protect it. Therefore I will not forsake my dharma lest it may annihilate me. (*Dharma eva hato hanti, dharmo rakshati rakshitah. Tasmāt dharmam na tyajāmi mā no dharmo hatovadhit).''*

(The motto of Vishva Hindu Parishad *dharmo rakshati rakshitah* comes from this verse.)

The *Yaksha*, who was Dharmarāj in disguise, was only testing *Yudhishthir*. He told him so and brought all the four brothers back to life.

From Neetishāstra

Hitopadesh and Panchtantra contain verses dealing with moral conduct, tactful behaviour, and statecraft. We quote here three verses to give a flavor for what they contain.

Asambhavam hema mrigasya janma,
tathāpi Rāmo lulubhe mrigāya
Prāyah samāpanna vipattikāle,
dhiyopi purushā malina bhavanti.

The birth of a golden deer is impossible, still Rāma was lured by the golden deer (Māreecha). Often, even the intellects of great men get dull when bad times are approaching.

Ati rupena haryo Sitā, ati garven Rāvana
Ati dānirbalirvaddho, ati sarvatra varjayet.

Sitā got abducted because of her excessive beauty. Rāvana got killed because of his excessive haughtiness. Bali got destroyed because of his excessive charitable habit. Therefore excess should be avoided in every walk of life.

Na sā Sabhā yatra na santi briddhā,
briddhā na te ye na vadanti dharmam
Dharmah sa no yatra na satyamasti,
satyam na tat yat chhalam ubhyapaiti.

A social gathering is not a gathering if there are no seniors (to provide guidance). Seniors are not seniors if their words are not consistent with the canons of dharma. Dharma is not dharma if it is not based on truth and truth does not coexist with deceit.

★ ★ ★

CATERING TO THE INTELLECT

A distinguishing characteristic of Hinduism is that it owes its origin not to faith but to wisdom gained through inquisitive mind and questioning intellect. The Upanishads, the cornerstone of Hinduism, reflect the process and outcome of the inquisitive mind. Whether or not a Hindu has seen or read the vedās or Purānās, his conduct and behavior are subconsciously affected by them because the culture is founded on them. They provide vitality to every fiber of our moral and spiritual life. Separated from the mainstream of our social and cultural background we tend to view our social and religious values more objectively. We feel compelled to question what we imbibed subconsciously, more so when a child growing up in our new social setup asks questions that we did not or could not ask our parents. Leaving aside some profound and fundamental questions, such as what is God, we should at least be able to explain to the inquisitive child the rationale behind the rituals, which we expect him to go through. We should be able to explain, for example, why Lord Ganesha has the head of an elephant or why most of the gods and goddesses have four hands.

It is an age-old practice to convey subtle ideas through stories. Any story has two aspects — the narrative and the ideas behind it. Hindu mythology, dispersed in Purānas and epics, was the outcome of an attempt to bring the abstract vedānta philosophy to the masses through lucid stories.

Although there are parts of some Purānas which are far from laudable, most of the stories have deep philosophical ideas interwoven in the simple narratives. On the surface the stories may seem frivolous, even ridiculous; they may even appear to insult one's intelligence. However, if one goes beyond the literal meaning of the narratives and delves into the symbolism behind the characters, a different picture emerges. Here we attempt to present some of the popular stories in that light.

Birth of Ganesha

(The story was narrated earlier in the text. This is a more detailed version from *Shiva Purāna*.)

Every worthwhile function in a traditional Hindu family starts with the invocation of Lord Ganesha. In keeping with the tradition, therefore, we begin with the story of the origin of Ganesha.

After their marriage Shiva and Pārvati lived in their home at Mount Kailāsh. Shiva was a wanderer by nature; he went out of and came back into the house at any odd hour. This caused much inconvenience to Pārvati and she was irked by frequent intrusions on her privacy. Devoted as she was to her husband she did not complain directly, but kept thinking about some way to guard her privacy. The household attendants were all ganas; they would not disobey or deter Shiva. She finally decided to have her own attendant who would obey her and her alone.

One day she collected the saffron paste flakes, which she had applied to her body for cleansing, and created a handsome young boy out of it. He looked strong and bright. She was so delighted that she immediately adopted him as her own son. Thus Pārvati got her *mānas putra* or the mind-born son. He became very devoted to his mother and would do anything for her. Until now, whenever Pārvati went to take a bath, she was always apprehensive of Shiva marching in without any regard for her privacy. But now she had her son to guard the door for her. She told him to guard the door and not let anyone in while she was bathing. The boy took a staff and sat guard at the door.

In a little while Shiva came back and was surprised to see a boy at the door barring his way. Shiva asked the boy who he was. On being told that he was mother Pārvati's son and nobody could enter the house while she was taking a bath, Shiva laughed and asked him to get out of his way, but the boy would not budge. This made Shiva furious and he proceeded to force his way; the boy resisted with incredible force surprising him. Shiva then ordered his *ganās* to get rid of the boy. The son was now in a dilemma; Shiva was his mother's lord, should he fight him and his *ganās*. He decided to put duty over feelings; ganās had to obey *Shiva's* orders, but he had to obey his mother. A fight ensued in which the *ganās* were defeated and fled. Surprised, Shiva brought the army of gods led by his son Kartikeya. A fierce battle followed and even the army could not vanquish the boy. Finally, in sheer desperation Shiva hurled his trident and severed the boy's head.

When Pārvati heard that the boy had been killed, she became furious and vowed that the gods including Shiva would pay for their deeds. She created thousands of *shaktis* including Kāli and Durgā and ordered them to destroy the gods and *ganās*. *Shaktis* proceeded to carry out her orders. There was pandemonium among the gods. *Brahmā* and *Vishnu* ran to *Pārvati* and asked her to have mercy on the gods. *Pārvati* demanded that her son must be restored to life and given an honorable status among the gods before she would stop the *Shaktis*. Brahmā and Vishnu then pleaded with Shiva to bring the boy back to life.

Meanwhile the severed head of the boy had disappeared,

perhaps taken away by some mountain creature. Shiva ordered his *ganās* to bring the head of the first child they found, whose mother was sleeping with face turned away from the child. Following the orders literally they brought the head of an elephant calf. Shiva fitted the head to the boy's body and brought him back to life. The gods were delighted and brought the boy to Pārvati. She was very unhappy though, thinking what will be the life of a boy growing up with human body and elephant's head. Shiva consoled her saying that the son would be blessed as the lord of *ganās* — Ganesha, and he would have a very privileged position among gods. In any function he would be worshipped before any other god. Thus was created Ganesha, the second son in the household of Shiva and Pārvati.

The philosophical aspect of the story spans the ideal bounds of human life. Earthly possessions or riches are important but only in a limited context. They are essentially as insignificant as the flakes of the saffron paste. In the ultimate union of the soul and the supreme reality (symbolized by the union of Shiva and Pārvati) there is no place for material things. They have to be done away with; that is the symbolism involved in the severance of the head. The material prosperity must be tempered by a faculty of discrimination between good and evil. One of these alone is not sufficient to take man to the exalted state; the two must coexist for the good of the individual and the society. The elephant is a symbol of material prosperity and well being. At the same time its wisdom and sense of discrimination are proverbial; it can find a needle in a haystack. The human body with elephant's head symbolizes the ideal combination of material prosperity and discriminating intellect. The two together spell success. Ganesha is the god of wealth and prosperity. He removes obstacles and guides the intellect in distinguishing between right and wrong.

An essential appendage to our mythological characters is *vāhan* which literally means carrier or in modern terminology a vehicle to transport the symbolic figure. The *vāhan* for Ganesha is the mouse, seemingly a very inappropriate one considering the heavy weight it has to carry. A mouse is small but it can devour many times its weight in no time. The traditional picture of Ganesha depicts the mouse with quivering tail looking at the sweets, not daring to touch them without permission. Desire and avarice, if not controlled can consume everything and lead a man to total destruction. On the other hand, controlled desire can lead to material prosperity and spiritual well-being

Pāndavas and Draupadi

The stories in the Purānas dealt primarily with different gods and goddesses. These were conjured up in the post-vedic era to bring the abstract vedānta philosophy within the grasp of the common man. The narratives were mainly at the supernatural plane. They lacked the continuity and cohesion of day to day events which the average person could relate to. The epics, drawing substance from the *Vedas* as well as *Purānas*, gave a historical perspective to the stories. Both Rāmāyana and Mahābhārata brought the philosophy closer to the common man who could identify himself, even if remotely, with the characters of the narrative and strive to emulate their role.

The plethora of stories contained in Mahābhārata have provided the sustaining framework to the structure of our moral life. There is not any aspect of human life that remains untouched there; it is in essence an extensive and exhaustive treatise on *vedānta* philosophy in the form of delicately interwoven stories. The philosophical implications of the stories are deep and subtle. The life of Pāndavas is the base on which this epic is built up. Naturally the symbolism of the underlying philosophy reaches its culmination when their lives end. This is perhaps one of the most beautiful aspects of Vyās' genius.

One of the most intriguing characters, at least from the point of view of society's norms and attitudes, is Draupadi with five husbands. As the narrative goes, Arjuna having won the hands of Draupadi in the *swayamvar* brings her to Kunti in the forest and tells her of his winning a prize. Without asking about the prize and without seeing Draupadi, Kunti unwittingly tells Arjuna to share the prize with his other four brothers. Most of us have accepted the story unquestioningly as Arjuna accepted his mother's words. However, we will now find it hard to explain the legitimacy of the action in the story to our young children. From a historical point of view we do not find any evidence of polyandry in vedic or post-vedic period. From Satyavati to Kunti to Draupadi, women have dominant roles in Mahābhārata. Why would Vyās then introduce an aberration in the character of Draupadi? To answer this question we have to look at the life of Pāndavas, their births and deaths. The apparent inconsistency of the story is the focal point of the philosophical symbolism of Mahābhārata.

Going back in the narrative to the origin of Pāndavas we recall that they were not born through the natural process of conception. Because of a curse upon Pāndu each one of them was conceived by Kunti through meditating on different gods. Yudhishthir was thus the progeny of Dharma, Bhima of Vāyu, Arjuna of Indra, and Nakul and Sahadeva of Ashvini Kumārs. The latter were *Mādri's* sons but they were also conceived through *Kunti's* meditation.

From birth to death the Pāndavas go through trials and

tribulations and come out victorious towards the end. It is time to quit.

After leaving the kingdom to their grandson Parikshit and the grandson in the charge of guru Kripāchārya, they together with Draupadi start on their final journey.

A dog comes along and joins them. They start walking north to Mount Meru. Soon Draupadi gets exhausted and drops dead by the wayside.

Seeing her fall Bhima asks Yudhishthir the cause of her helpless end despite being sinless.

Yudhishthir replies : "Although extremely pious and devoted, she had special preference for Arjuna and that was the reason for her sad demise."

A little farther Sahadeva falls and dies.

Again Bhima asks his elder brother the cause of this death.

The reply : "His ego. He never considered anyone as learned and intelligent as himself."

Seeing Draupadi and Sahadeva dropping dead Nakul is overcome with grief and dies.

To Bhima's question to Yudhishthir the answer is : "Nakul had his ego of being unmatched in physical beauty."

A little later Arjuna falters and dies; the answer to the same question : Arjuna's ego about his skill with weapons.

After a little distance Bhima himself feels his feet giving way and he asks why he was dying ?

Yudhishthir replied : "Because of your ego about your physical strength and your lack of consideration for others while eating." At this point only Yudhishthir kept going followed by the dog.

Soon Indra appeared with his golden chariot and asked Yudhishthir to step in to be taken to heaven without casting off his body.

Yudhishthir said :

"O king of gods, my brothers and Draupadi have fallen

dead along the way. Please arrange for them to be taken to heaven. I don't want to go to heaven without them".

Indra replied:

"They are already in heaven, you will meet them there."

Yudhishthir then told Indra : "The dog had been very faithful to me and should come with me."

Indra replied that there was no place for a dog in heaven and he would have to leave the dog behind.

Yudhishthir said that the dog had come under his protection and he would not forsake his duty and leave the dog behind. He would rather forego his place in heaven.

Indra said :

"O king, you left your brothers and dear Draupadi behind. How come you have more attachment to this dog?"

"O king of gods, I did not forsake them; I left behind their dead bodies. There can not be any attachment to dead bodies. The dog is alive and I can not forsake him. That is final."

At this point Dharmarāj, who was all along disguised as the dog, made himself manifest and praised Yudhishthir for his infallible adherence to duty and they all proceeded to heaven.

Let us now get back to the central figure of this discussion — Draupadi. She was also called *Pānchāli*; the word *Pānchāli* means one pervaded by the five elements, i.e. the manifest world. The enjoyer of the world is *jiva* or *man*. *Man* is made up of five basic entities: the physical body, the *prān vāyu*, the mind, the intellect and the soul. Draupadi symbolizes the material world. Her enjoyer or husband is one but made up of five constituent entities; Yudhishthir born of Dharma represents the soul (ātmā); Bhima born of Vāyu represents the *prā*n; Arjuna was born of Indra representing mind (*man*); Nakul and Sahadeva born of Ashvinikumārs represent respectively the physical body and the intellect.

Symbolically the five Pāndavas constitute one man and, hence, one husband; Draupadi is a symbolic ideal woman, wife of that symbolic ideal person.

We now consider the sequence of events that take place when a man is dying. He first loses his capacity to enjoy the worldly things — Draupadi dies. Then the intellect gets fogged — Sahadeva dies. Next his body stops functioning—Nakul goes. This is followed by the mind stopping its function — Arjuna dies. Finally the life itself, i.e. *prān* goes — Bhima dies. The soul is indestructible — Yudhishthir remains unfaltering. The only thing which goes with the soul is karma — the faithful dog keeps following Yudhishthir. Viewed in this context the inconsistency of *Draupadi's* characterization disappears as do many other inconsistencies when Mahābhārata is taken as a battle between the forces of good and evil within the human body symbolized by Kurukshetra.

Satyanārāyana Vrat Kathā

Hinduism is not a faith, it is a way of life. From birth to death religion is inseparably mingled with day to day life. It will be hard to find clear demarcating lines between social and religious activities.

The mythological stories play a significant role in all such activities directly or indirectly. Perhaps the most popular among these is *Satyanārāyana Vrat Kathā*, taken from Skand Purāna. The complete story used in traditional poojā consists of five chapters of Revākhand. However, the main part of the story is contained in the third and fourth chapters, which is summarized here.

In early times there was a king named Ulkāmukh. He was very learned, wise and truthful. He went to the temple daily. He had a beautiful and faithful wife named Pramugdhā. They regularly worshipped Lord *Satyanārāyana* at the banks of Bhadrashilā river. Once while they were performing *poojā*, a businessman named Sādhu arrived there by boat. He came to the king and asked what he was doing. The king replied that he was worshipping Lord Satyanārāyana for obtaining progeny. Sādhu requested the king to kindly explain the rituals to him, since he also did not have any child. The king obliged.

Returning home from the trip Sādhu narrated the incident to his wife Lilāvati. He made a solemn resolve to perform *Satyanārāyana Vrat* if they were blessed with a child. Within the year they had a beautiful daughter, they named her Kalāvati. Lilāvati reminded her husband of his resolve to perform the poojā. He said that he would perform the poojā at the time of Kalāvati's marriage and again went on his business trip. When Kalāvati came of age, he found a suitable young man of his own profession and performed the daughter's marriage. Unfortunately he forgot his resolve of performing the poojā. Accompanied by his son-in-law he again set out on a business trip. Lord Satyanārāyana got annoyed and decided to teach Sādhu a lesson.

Sādhu and his son-in-law were doing good business in the kingdom of Chandraketu. One day some thieves, being pursued by the king's soldiers, hid the stolen goods in the place where Sādhu was staying. The two were arrested and all their earnings were confiscated.

Meanwhile Lilāvati and her daughter were also suffering. They had been robbed; they were sick and constantly worried about their husbands. One day, troubled by hunger, Kalāvati went to the temple where a group of people were performing *S*atyanārāyana poojā. She sat there and listened to the narrator. She felt very happy and told her mother about it. Lilāvati immediately decided to perform the poojā. After the poojā she begged the Lord for the safe return of her husband and son-in-law. Pleased with her the

Lord commanded king Chandraketu in his dream to let the two out of his jail and return their wealth adding an equal amount from his own treasury.

The two men set out for the return journey, their boat loaded with money and merchandise. The Lord wanted to test if Sādhu had learned any humility. He appeared disguised as a monk and asked him what they had in their boat?

The businessman said laughingly :

"Do you want money? There are only leaves and branches in my boat."

The monk said : "So be it" and disappeared.

After a while when the businessmen looked at their boat they could not believe what they saw. The boat did not show any sign of holding any weight as if it really were loaded with leaves. Sādhu fainted at the thought of losing his fortune again. When he came around, his son-in-law suggested that the monk was really the Lord in disguise and he should not have slighted him. They both ran to find the monk and saw him sitting not far away. The businessman fell at his feet and begged to be forgiven. With the Lord's blessing they found the boat restored with its original contents. Then and there they collected together all their men and performed Satyanārāyana poojā in proper manner and continued their journey home.

When they arrived at their hometown Sādhu wished to see his wife and daughter at the bank of the river so that they could enter the town together. He sent a message to his wife. Both mother and daughter were performing Satyanārāyana poojā. After completing poojā the mother hurried to meet her husband instructing the daughter to follow as soon as she completed her fast. In her eagerness to see her husband, Kalāvati forgot to take Lord's offering (*prasād*). The Lord got annoyed with her negligence and made the boat go underwater. Kalāvati's husband was still on the boat.

When Kalāvati did not see her husband she fainted with shock. Her father was dumb with fear and started wondering what happened. Lilāvati started crying not knowing if the boat had capsized or just disappeared. Meanwhile Kalāvati regained consciousness and started walking into the river to end her life. At this point Sādhu and his wife sensed the hand of Lord Satyanārāyana in shaping these events and, praying to him, they resolved to perform Satyanārāyana Vrat again. The Lord was propitiated and told them that their daughter had neglected his offering in her haste to see her husband; that was the reason for their misfortune. If she went home and returned after taking prasād, she would immediately see her husband. Hearing this Kalāvati ran home and returned after taking prasād. She was delighted to see her husband waiting for her. They all went home and thereafter performed Satyanārāyana Vrat every full moon.

Looking at the narrative alone it seems rather crude. In spite of being the most popular of the Purānic stories it is unlikely to appeal to the intellect. The concept of God as an omnipotent, kind and benevolent Being is all but shattered when one finds that seemingly trivial incidents can arouse in Him extreme wrath as well as benevolence. Perhaps such stories were written partly to arouse devotion through fear but it would be wrong to see this as the whole motive. Let us examine this story in a different light.

Lord Satyanārāyana is, of course, the focal point of the story just as Brahman is the focal point of all Upanishads. He represents the eternal truth. The word 'lilā' in Sanskrit means sport and is often taken to be synonymous with *māyā*. Thus Liāvati symbolizes personification of *māyā*. *Sādhu*, the businessman is a symbolic figure representing any common man or *jeeva*. With the blessing of God the union of *jiva* and *māyā* produces *kalā*; *kalā* is a word representing all the fine attributes or art forms perceived in the manifest world. Thus Kalāvati represents personification of all such attributes. The enjoyer of *kalā* is the soul and *kalā* can find identification only with the soul, represented by the son-in-law. *Ketu* is supposed to swallow the moon during eclipse. Chandraketu jails the two men and turns all the happiness of Kalāvati and Lilāvati into misery.

The chief blessing of Lord Satyanārāyana is truth; that is his *prasād*. The performance of *poojā* and *vrat* amounts to observance of truth. Neglect of truth leads to unhappiness in different forms symbolized by different, apparently inconsistent incidents in the story. The neglect of prasād by Kalāvati in her haste to meet her husband symbolizes the disregard of truth in the pursuit of daily duties. When 'kalā' does not reflect truth, it loses its beauty and no longer appeals to the soul — there is no enjoyer. Thus Kalāvati does not see her husband — he disappears. When truth is regained by *kalā* it delights the soul — Kalāvati's husband reappears.

The worship and rituals are a means by which man can condition himself for continual improvement. They are steps that can lead to higher and higher stages of life. Even if one first inculcates devotion to God for selfish motives, one gets conditioned to seek selfless devotion. To start on the path of devotion even with the hope of gaining material benefits is better than not starting at all. Sooner or later the selfish motives drop by the wayside.

★ ★ ★